VARIATION AND FIXITY IN NATURE

VARIATION AND FIXITY IN NATURE

The Meaning of Diversity and Discontinuity
in the World of Living Things, and
Their Bearing on Creation and Evolution

By Frank L. Marsh, MS, PhD
Author of *Fundamental Biology, Evolution, Creation,
and Science, Studies in Creationism,
Life, Man, and Time,*
and *Evolution or Special Creation?*

PUBLISHERS
Eugene, Oregon

Wipf and Stock Publishers
199 West 8th Avenue, Suite 3
Eugene, Oregon 97401

Variation and Fixity in Nature
The Meaning of Diversity and Discontinuity in the World of Living Things,
and their Bearing on Creation and Evolution
By Marsh, Frank L.
Copyright©1976 by Marsh, Frank L.
ISBN: 1-59244-718-X
Publication date: 5/26/2004
Previously published by Pacific Press Publishing Association, 1976

CONTENTS

1. Variation Everywhere   7
2. The Species, Real or Imaginary?   13
3. Species and the Genesis Kind   25
4. The Physical Basis of Heredity   42
5. Causes of Variation in Organisms   49
6. Hybridization   67
7. What Does the Fossil Record Tell Us?   80
8. Fixity Among Living Things   87
9. The Form and Structure of Living Things   92
10. Thoughts to Ponder   118
    Glossary   125
    References   141
    Index   145

CHAPTER 1

Variation Everywhere

Variety is truly the spice of life. If we doubt the truth of the adage, we have only to imagine what it would be to live in a world in which all men looked alike, all women looked alike, all cats, dogs, and horses looked alike. Likewise all houses, cars, trees, flowers, birds, insects, and even sunsets.

Variation in the natural world is so omnipresent that we recognize it as one of the invariable facts in nature. We do not see two identical leaves on a tree or two exactly equal clouds in the sky. Nor do we expect to. From remotest times man has tried to discover and understand the significance of this diversity.

As we study variation in nature, we soon discover another universal fact—the *discontinuity* of diversity among plants and animals. Living things in their multitudinous varieties cannot be arranged in a continuous unbroken series from simplest in structure to most complex, nor can one variant be traced through a continuous series to a markedly different variant. Instead, we observe that the variation is discontinuous. Rather than a graded series of individuals, we find separate clusters of similar forms. This fact makes it possible, with the greatest of ease, to distinguish among our domesticated plants and animals. We know the horses from the cows, the cats from the dogs, the roses from the camellias, the corn from the wheat, the maples from the oaks. This discontinuity has made possible the construction of scientific classifications of living things, and the discontinuous clusters have been assigned the terms *phylum, class, order, family, genus,* and *species.*

Depending on our understanding of origins, classification of living things can mean different things to different people. In the mind of the creationist, basic kinds of living things came into existence by the spoken word of a Supreme Being. To the creationist, then, no genetic relationship exists between basic kinds because each was produced separately from all others by an act of creation. If, on the other hand, the student believes that over a period of some 600 million years a Supreme Being through a manipulation of natural processes, derived the more complex basic kinds from the simpler kinds, then similarity of structure would indicate genetic relationship. Again, if the student is inclined toward mechanism and disallows a Supreme Being, to him any similarity in appearance of one group to another would suggest genetic relationship.

Whatever the student's point of view, we will find that the grouping of natural clusters into some classification plan will be essential as a matter of convenience in referring to this or that category. We must remember, however, that taxonomic groupings, with the possible exception of the major groups, the phyla, are largely arbitrary, and the arrangement of groups in classification systems may be mostly for convenience in handling thousands and even millions of names. R. A. Pimental, English taxonomist, recognized the gulf between the studied sample and the living population and maintained that "most proposals of taxa below the genus are little more than hypothesis."[1] This classification of organisms is a recognition of the fact of discontinuity. Horses have a number of morphological characteristics in common with cows, yet at the same time

VARIATION EVERYWHERE

the absence of intermediate, intergrading forms sets them apart as clearly as two separate islands in the sea.

As we consider the impressive fact of variation in nature, we find a great deal of difference between the *extent of variation* of individuals within one group when compared with that within some other group. When we study specimens of such clusters as the American eel, some of the chalcid wasps, the thistle butterfly, the garden weed purslane, and the ginkgo or maidenhair tree, we find that within their respective groups all the individuals are at least superficially identical. In each such case a stability of organization is present which prevents rearrangement within germ cells of individuals of the cluster.

However, in most of our domesticated plants and animals, many contrasting and somewhat unstable factors exist in their gene pools. For example, there are varieties in the horse group as different as race horses and work horses, ponies and Percherons, asses and zebras. Within the cattle group are milk cows and beef cattle, buffalo and zebus. In plants we see springing from the single gene pool of corn (maize) forms as diverse as dent, flint, starch (flour), sweet, waxy, pop, and pod. And have you ever tried to count the variants within the sweet corn type alone? If that has swamped you, turn to the bean cluster and tell the number of varieties of beans in the world. Furthermore if you weary of plants and animals, try counting the distinct breeds within mankind. One human ecologist thought he could distinguish 160 distinct breeds of men on the earth.[2]

With this plethora of varieties within any one cluster of discontinuous groups, we must not lose sight of the fact that *in not even one instance has the production of a new, discrete cluster or kind as different as a horse and a cow been known.* In the horse cluster every variant is unmistakably a horse; in the human cluster every breed of man is unmistakably a human being; and so on. This is a universal fact of tremendous significance. It is easy for us to say, "Of course," without perceiving what this actual performance in nature means relative to the problem of origins.

When referring to the production of subspecies, varieties, or breeds within species, many scientists in the last few decades have come to use the term *microevolution*. Its opposite is *macroevolution*. "Microevolution" is used to designate a process easily observed by all of us. "Macroevolution" refers to the evolutionists' assumption that complex and specialized basic types of plants and animals have developed from simpler, more generalized types. This point of view should be rated, not as fact, but as a hypothesis; the production of even one new basic type by a different one has yet to be demonstrated in nature.

Thus if a dog kind could produce a cat kind, or if an ape kind could produce a man kind, we would have the macroevolution type of change. Changes so large still remain entirely in the realm of the speculative, the philosophical, having been demonstrated neither from fossils nor in the living world. On the other hand, in living our lives day by day we are surrounded with examples of microevolution as we recognize the multitudinous breeds of dogs, the many varieties of pigeons, and the varieties of roses ranging from a pure white scented rose through cream, yellow, orange, lavender, to red and finally a black-red scentless rose.

Dobzhansky,[3] the late noted geneticist, has differentiated between the use of these terms, microevolution and macroevolution, stating that the former includes the evolutionary processes observable within the span of a human lifetime as distinguished from the latter, which is observable only on a geological scale. We may add that he makes the latter assertion only hopefully rather than upon the basis of laboratory evidence.

VARIATION EVERYWHERE

In one of his volumes, the outstanding geneticist Goldschmidt stated it to "be one of the major contentions of this book to show that the facts of microevolution do not suffice for an understanding of macroevolution. The latter term will be used here for the evolution of the good species and all the higher taxonomic categories."[4] The increasing use of these terms, largely in biological circles, is evidenced in that the words "microevolution" and "macroevolution" appeared in the addenda to the 1953 printing of *Webster's New International Dictionary*, Second Edition; however, they appear in the main body of the Third Edition (1961).

If all biologists viewed the origin of plants and animals from the point of view of evolution, possibly the terms microevolution and macroevolution would satisfy the great majority of them. But because of many special creationists, saltationists, orthogeneticists, Lamarckians, and others, there is considerable dissatisfaction with these terms. Interestingly, from a search of the literature, it appears that the word "evolution" was first used by a creationist, the Swiss naturalist Charles Bonnet (1720-1793), in his preformation or incasement theory, according to which succeeding generations were all created in a beginning as germs inside the body of the first parent. Then, as the time came for another generation to develop, the germ unrolled ("evolved") into an adult.

The creationist wishes a word other than microevolution could be used when referring to variation within the species because, through usage, "evolution" suggests the development of new basic groups never known before. Creationists broaden the term microevolution to include all variation within a basic kind or type. Because of the use of the term "microevolution" to cover variation within the species—a common biological phenomenon—the creationist becomes by definition a "microevolutionist."

This terminology may be confusing to some.

Microevolution, then, is variation occurring within the basic type. Macroevolution is the hypothetical bridging from one species (using "species" in the sense of a basic type of organism) to a new basic type. Both terms actually hang upon the definition of *species*. We shall attempt to define this term in the next chapter. In some respects the problem of origins hinges on semantics, the meaning of words.

CHAPTER 2

The Species, Real or Imaginary?

In order to progress in our study of origins we must first endeavor to understand what group of organisms the evolutionist refers to by the term "species." In definitions of both micro- and macroevolution we find that, to understand either type of evolution, we must first define the term *species*. The evolutionist defines microevolution as *intraspecific* variation (appearance of new subspecies, breeds, or varieties within the species), while he defines macroevolution as *interspecific* variation (variation assumed to be of such magnitude and quality as to result in the production of a completely new species).

At this point we may be tempted to think, This is going to be easy. All we have to do to learn if organic evolution has occurred is to review the changes observable in species. If we find that one species has given rise to a new species, then macroevolution has occurred.

Unfortunately, things are not so easy as we attempt to find out what biologists mean when they say "species." The English creationist naturalist John Ray (1627?-1705) seems to have been the first man to become aware of clusters of individuals in nature which he called "species."[1] In his view, plants belonged to the same species if through their seed they produced a new plant similar to themselves. In his opinion the same principle prevailed among animals. Ray believed that God had created the species, and that no new species could arise because God completed His work (rested from it) with the close of the sixth day, the last working day of Creation week. Ray was aware of variation in some species, a phenomenon which he attributed to "degeneration" of seeds. With the exception of Ray, most naturalists of the pre-Linnaean period believed in the transmutation of species. They believed that from the seed of one kind of plant, say a radish, a quite different kind of plant, say a carrot, might spring forth.

One important work of the Swedish creationist Carolus Linnaeus (1707-1778), father of modern taxonomy, was his disproof of transmutation in nature by showing the objectivity and constancy of species. Through his influence the idea of spontaneous generation of higher organisms ended. During the earlier part of his active working period, Linnaeus believed that "there are as many species as there were originally created diverse forms,"[2] and he endeavored to assign species names to the clusters of organisms which he thought were the Genesis kinds. In his assignment of species names he tried to include all individuals in the same species which could breed with one another to produce fertile offspring. Possibly because of the lack of information in his day regarding what forms could cross, he frequently gave a separate species name to a cluster of individuals we now know could cross with other clusters. Examples are his separate species names for the horse (*Equus caballus* L.), the ass (*E. asinus* L.), and the zebra (*E. zebra* L.)[3] We now know these to be varieties of a single horse kind, as they are frequently cross-fertile.[4] Linnaeus likewise considered as separate species the American bison (*Bison bison* L.), European bison (*Bison bonasus* L.), and cattle (*Bos taurus* L.). Hybrids between these two bison and the true cattle are usually quite fertile.

THE SPECIES, REAL OR IMAGINARY?

Linnaeus also made some puzzling decisions in his naming of plants. In his endeavor to include interfertile individuals in a single group, he commonly served as a "lumper"—lumping diverse kinds together. In other cases he appeared as a "splitter," assigning separate species names to spring wheat (*Triticum aestivum* L.) and winter wheat (*T. hybernum* L.).[5] Although these strains of wheat and others will all cross and produce fertile hybrids, Linnaeus, to our confusion, considered them separate species.

Linnaeus was handicapped by more than lack of information on hybridization. He also attempted the difficult task of classifying biological species in the living world while at the same time, for the convenience of the taxonomist, indicating objective species in the laboratory. His problems suggest that possibly taxonomists today should develop two different systems in classification, one for biological groups among living plants and animals in the field, and one for convenience in designating smaller groups within the large cross-fertile populations. The latter could be based on morphological characters without concern about possible genetic relationships. For example, *Bos taurus* can be conveniently distinguished from *Bison bison*, even though they are unquestionably members of the same basic type of animal. Might we say, the same biological species?

As a special creationist, Linnaeus believed the Bible to be a book of truth from Genesis to Revelation. He understood as fact and truth the Genesis narration of the origin of plants: "And God said, 'Let the earth put forth vegetation, plants yielding seed, and fruit trees bearing fruit in which is their seed, each according to its kind, upon the earth.' And it was so. The earth brought forth vegetation, plants yielding seed according to their own kinds, and trees bearing fruit in which is their seed, each according to its kind. And God saw that it was good." Genesis 1:11, 12, RSV.

Because of the biblical portrayal of kinds of plants as self-reproducing units in nature, Linnaeus attempted to assign species names to intrafertile clusters much as the Linnaean taxonomists of our day attempt to do. As already noted, Linnaeus assigned some of his species names to clusters which could cross with other species clusters. These seemed to cause him concern, and in his declining years he carried on rather extensive hybridization experiments. He finally concluded that he had, in his earlier efforts to discover the Genesis kinds, often set his species locus too low and too narrow. It was his mature opinion that the originally created Genesis kinds were units which he called "orders." He speculated that God had crossed these to produce families, and these in turn hybridized in nature to produce genera.[6] Of course, to get a clear concept of Linnaeus's mature opinion, the student would have to become acquainted with the groups in his classification system, a system made up of only four categories—the class, the order, the genus, and the species.

Regardless of how confusing to us Linnaeus's final view may be, we must give him credit for sensing that very real natural groupings do exist, which are distinguished primarily by their ability to cross. That is, in keeping with Genesis, it appears that he thought the real differences among living things resided in their internal chemistry instead of in different morphological patterns—they brought forth after their own kinds. Of course we know that the chemistry of the genes determines the morphology. However, male and female of the same animal may differ drastically in appearance, as illustrated in the marine worm *Bonellia*, where the female may be three feet in length while the male lives as a tiny parasite in her nephridial system.

The positive influence of Linnaeus toward the concept of constancy and objectivity of the species was accepted by

THE SPECIES, REAL OR IMAGINARY?

most scientists for almost a century, until Darwin's *Origin of Species* came from the press in 1859. Darwin apparently made a common mistake when he sought to identify the species in nature, by focusing his attention at too low a level. He permitted himself to become distracted by ecological and geographical varieties of such clusters as tortoises and finches, thus missing the tremendously important fact that all the varieties of finches were still unquestionably finches, and those of the tortoises were still 100 percent tortoises. The true species he was seeking existed at the level of the Galápagos tortoise and not at the level of its varieties. With all his powers of keen observation, he failed to comprehend that this tortoise was a true, enduring entity in nature from which no amount of internal variation could produce a new basic type.

Darwin's principal contribution to science was his publicizing the fact that variation does occur in nature. During the Middle Ages certain theologians had done biology a great disservice by misrepresenting Genesis. The Bible record, they said, taught that living things could not vary because they brought forth after their kinds, and this meant that each generation would be identical to the one before it, like coins stamped from the same die. In the face of this interpretation of Genesis by Cambridge schoolmen, Darwin pointed out that plants and animals *do* vary somewhat from their progenitors. Furthermore, after Darwin had called attention to the phenomenon, even the man in the street could see that he was right—domesticated plants and animals often *do* appear in many varieties. The tragedy is that when Darwin demonstrated the inaccuracy of the *scholastic interpretation* of Genesis, he thought he had disproved *Genesis*. (Any one of us can read Genesis for ourselves, and we will discover no assertion that the created kind cannot vary within itself.)

18 VARIATION AND FIXITY IN NATURE

One evolutionist has written: "Darwin, who had started the voyage of the *Beagle* with views similar to those of Agassiz [a creationist], began to think seriously about evolution only after he had found overwhelming evidence that was completely irreconcilable with the idea of an origin of the world fauna and flora by creation."[7] The kindest thing we can say about this comment is that it is narrowly dogmatic, because it considers only one explanation to be possible. When Darwin began this five-year voyage, the only theory of creation he knew was the narrow scholastic interpretation of Genesis stressing invariability of plants and animals.

According to Genesis, in the beginning the earth was populated with plants and animals in all their distinct kinds. The plants reproductively yielded "seed according to their own kinds." Genesis 1:12, RSV. "On the sixth day God completed all the work He had been doing" (Genesis 2:2, NEB), including the population of the earth with discrete kinds of plants and animals. Some seventeen centuries later, because of confusion accompanying the entrance of sin, all *land animals* were drowned in a universal deluge, the only survivors being those saved in Noah's ark. Genesis 7:19-23. After the Flood the animals disembarked in the "mountains of Ararat," and from that area dispersed over the entire earth. Genesis 8:4, 17, 19.

The doctrine of special creation is founded upon the biblical references given in the above paragraph. If Darwin and the systematist referred to above had thoughtfully read for themselves this account upon which the creationist doctrine is based, they would find not even one item of natural evidence "completely irreconcilable with the idea of an origin of the world fauna and flora by creation." As long as organisms bring forth according to their own kinds (no laboratory findings show any exception to this principle),

THE SPECIES, REAL OR IMAGINARY? 19

the scientific evidence on variation harmonizes with Genesis. The scientist who sincerely seeks truth in nature will not refuse any pertinent hypothesis until he has measured it with demonstrable facts. We recognize the great powers of observation possessed by Darwin, but we are amazed that he did not observe the limits of variation. Variation, he should have recognized, can produce new varieties only within kinds already in existence—a situation which could never result in organic evolution. While tracing migration paths of plants and animals, Darwin never grasped the fact that *he was able to trace those routes because the migrants were still bona fide members of the same basic kinds to which their ancestors belonged.*

Darwin, then, thought he had proved the Bible inaccurate, and having broken away from the scholastic interpretation of Genesis, he lost interest in Christianity. Reacting against the extreme view of no variation between generations, he swung to the opposite and equally inaccurate view that variation in plants and animals proceeds without limit. The longer Darwin turned this idea over in his mind, the more attractive the concept of endless progression became, until he was completely sold on the hypothesis of organic evolution. Then having convinced himself of this fantasy, he proceeded to convince others—and Darwin was an excellent salesman. In a way which seems beyond natural explanation, his portrayal of limitless progression laid hold upon the imaginations of scientist and layman alike. Darwin's followers have succeeded in promoting the idea so completely that scientists, to save the hypothesis, have patched and repatched the patches. Neo-Darwinism now bears small resemblance to Darwin's original portrayal, except that it holds to the idea of unlimited change.

Darwin actually started out to discover the origin of species. But as his faith in the occurrence of evolution increased, he elaborated a theory of continual minute variations winnowed by natural selection. He became convinced that it was impossible to bound, or discover, the loci of species. His lack of understanding of the nature of species is revealed in the following statements: "I look at the term species as one arbitrarily given, for the sake of convenience, to a set of individuals closely resembling each other, and that it does not essentially differ from the term variety, which is given to less distinct and more fluctuating forms." Again, "In determining whether a form should be ranked as a species or a variety, the opinion of naturalists having sound judgment and wide experience seems the only guide to follow."[8] Thus by denying the existence of nonarbitrary species as natural units, Darwin eliminated the need of explaining how species multiply.

After the appearance of Darwin's *Origin of Species* in 1859, biologists divided themselves into two camps: those who chose to follow Linnaeus's concept of reality and objectivity of species, and those who with Darwin chose to accept the concept of nonexistence of concrete, discrete species, focusing their attention on individuals as the essential units of evolution. The evolutionist taxonomist Mayr goes to some pains to explain how, in his opinion, the recognition of clearly demarked species in nature does not deny evolution: "There is no conflict between the fact of evolution and the fact of the clear delimitation of species in a local flora or fauna."[9]

Since the time of Darwin, and largely through Darwinism, a great deal of confusion has existed among authorities with regard to the nature of species. Geneticists, plant breeders, other experimental biologists, together with taxonomists, commonly tend to minimize the reality of species. Darwin's judgment that "whether a form should be ranked as a species or a variety, the opinion of naturalists having sound

THE SPECIES, REAL OR IMAGINARY?

judgment and wide experience seems the only guide to follow," seems to be the accepted guideline.

During the first half of the present century the best definition of a species ran something like this: A species is a systematic unit which is considered a species by a competent systematist. Crossability has been of small concern to most taxonomists, as they work within four walls well removed from the field situation. It must be a real disappointment to the morphological taxonomist to be forced to refrain from assigning separate species names to some breeds of dogs, horses, and even men. Because we are so well acquainted with the entire population in such cases, and are familiar with crossability among the dogs, horses, and men, our knowledge requires that within each kind all individuals be assigned to a single species. Lack of information concerning the actual crossability of most forms still leaves the morphological taxonomist quite free in the assignment of new species names. For the insect world alone a number of new morphological species are added to the list almost every day of the year.

Our taxonomic lists today hold every type of species from biological (for example, man, a single species, *Homo sapiens* L., including forms as diverse as the tall, fair-skinned Nordics and the dwarf, yellow, leathery-skinned bushmen) to minutely morphological species (such forms as species of ladybird beetles, *Coccinellidae*, which may vary only in color of the wing covers and the number and arrangement of spots on their backs).

The use of minute morphological characters in species determination was formerly made among such forms as the foxes, such as the Newfoundland Red Fox with its pale colors and the Western Red Fox with its large size, long tail, and rich colors.[10] To the confusion of the student, separate *species* names were early assigned to ten *varieties* of red foxes by Merriam, Bangs, Desmarest, Rhoads, DeKay, and Baird. However, Hall and Kelson now list one species of red fox, *Vulpes fulva,* consisting of twelve subspecies.[11] In this case the earlier taxonomists were splitters while Hall and Kelson might be classed as lumpers. A true lumper would not even have recognized the former species as subspecies of his single new species. Lumpers endeavor to keep our classification lists as short as possible.

In the plant kingdom, a shining example of a splitter is Sturtevant's assignment of a species name to each variety of corn (now known collectively as *Zea mays*). His species names, once used quite widely, were interestingly apt: Pod corn, *Zea tunicata;* popcorn, *Z. everta;* dent corn, *Z. indentata;* flour corn, *Z. amylacea;* flint corn, *Z. indurata;* and sweet corn, *Z. saccharata.*[12] Sturtevant's species are now considered to be breeds, or at most subspecies of a single species, *Z. mays.* Because Linnaeus included all corn under a single species name, he was in that case a lumper. Because Sturtevant divided the breeds of corn into six species, he is thought of as a splitter.

Although the cases of foxes and corn have been clarified by placing all varieties of red foxes into one species, *Vulpes fulva,* and by placing all varieties of corn into Linnaeus's single species, *Zea mays,* the fact remains that our lists present a confusion of splitter species (also called Jordanian for the French botanist Jordan, who pioneered this type of splitting in the early 1800s), and lumper species (also called Linnaean for Carolus Linnaeus, who with John Ray pioneered this type of lumping in the 1700s). One can imagine the confusion of the student of origins! What is meant by "species"? Are we talking about Jordanian or Linnaean species? If the former, then "evolution" has occurred because by controlled breeding new Jordanian species can be produced.

THE SPECIES, REAL OR IMAGINARY?

Walker[13] lists seven species of true cattle (genus *Bos*) as follows: Domesticated cattle, *B. taurus;* the zebu, *B. indicus;* the yak or grunting ox, *B. grunniens;* the gaur, *B. gaurus;* the gayal, *B. frontalis;* the banteng, *B. banteng;* and the kouprey, *B. sauveli.* We assume that biologically these true cattle have been assigned scientific names by splitter taxonomists, because they either are known to hybridize or are thought to be capable of doing so. One of the most recent breeds of *Bos* to gain official recognition is the Santa Gertrudis, obtained by breeding zebu bulls, *B. indicus,* with stock developed from strains of *B. taurus* (Texas longhorns, Herefords, and shorthorns). If the species of Walker's genus *Bos* are "true species," then the new breed Santa Gertrudis is just as defensibly a new species as Walker's are species. If so, then macroevolution has been accomplished, by definition, through a process of microevolution. Such are the tricky semantics involved in the present-day discussion of the problem of origins.

However, the development of Santa Gertrudis from a cross of *Bos taurus* with *B. indicus* is *not* true evolution. No new basic type has appeared, because Santa Gertrudis is unquestionably still a member of true cattle (Walker's genus *Bos*). In the increasingly popular modern viewpoint, Santa Gertrudis is not a new species, because it is freely crossfertile with *B. taurus.* This sort of change, according to all empirical evidence, can never result in organic evolution. The most that microevolution can produce is new Jordanian species, ie, new varieties within the fox kind, the cow kind, the corn kind, and the like. Within the living world and the world of fossils not one case of *known* macroevolution can be found. We must always remember that speculative science is not empirical science, not "coercive" science.

Science consists of a demonstrable portion stockpiled by laboratory evidence and observation, and a speculative portion erected upon hypotheses and theories which endeavor to interpret the demonstrated facts of empirical science. Both special creationists and evolutionists accept demonstrable facts. It is in the realm of the speculative where they part company. Every scientist must keep clearly in mind which is a demonstrable fact and which is merely speculative. He who becomes confused and begins to think that speculative items for his point of view are demonstrable facts has become a liability to those who search for natural truth. Such a case was painfully evident at the Darwin Centennial Celebration in Chicago in 1959 when a noted scientist became overfilled with the effulgence of his point of view and proclaimed that organic evolution is now as completely demonstrated a fact as the sphericity of our earth. This popular physical scientist illustrates a very common confusion of the speculative with the empirical. Such confusion impedes true natural science.

We have yet to consider the viewpoint of those who feel that species are real, concrete units in nature. This we shall discuss in the next chapter.

CHAPTER 3

Species and the Genesis Kind

It appears that the English naturalist Ray (1686) and the Swedish taxonomist Linnaeus (1738) were the first biologists to recognize the reproductive gap (inability to cross) as the mechanism in nature which results in discontinuity of forms in the living world, demarking one species from another. Ray seems to have made all his species designations upon this principle; while Linnaeus, though recognizing the reproductive gaps among living plants and animals, often assigned different species names to two or more interfertile populations. It would appear that Ray's species were always biological, while those of Linnaeus were sometimes biological and often morphological, determined in plants by such characters as the number of stamens and divisions of the pistil.

We have called attention to the situation among classifiers in the past in which each expert assigned new species names to any cluster of individuals which he felt rated such distinction. This was confusing not only to biologists in general but also to taxonomists themselves. To obviate such confusion in recent decades specialists have tried to find a standard yardstick on which there could be general agreement.

Most interestingly, in recent decades there has been a trend among evolutionist biologists toward acceptance of a combining species designation often referred to as a "biological species" definition. It is based on the reproductive gap which is discoverable between two discrete clusters of individuals, and upon the concept of the common gene pool of each intrafertile cluster. Thus the species leaves the ranks of dead, dried, pressed, and stuffed specimens and becomes a living population of active entities which produce fertile offspring, drawing their hereditary factors from a single source, a common gene pool. Nearly all species definitions of the last fifty years include directly or indirectly some reference to these two elements, the gap and the pool. The late Dobzhansky[1] appears to have been the first geneticist (1935) to define the species in these terms.

Other recent definitions of the biological species follow the same theme. Mayr defined it as "groups of actually or potentially interbreeding natural populations which are reproductively isolated from other such groups."[2] In a recent volume he defined it again: "Species [biological] are groups of interbreeding natural populations that are reproductively isolated from other such groups."[3] According to Simpson, "a genetic species is a group of organisms so constituted and so situated in nature that a hereditary character of any one of these organisms may be transmitted to a descendent of any other."[4] Dobzhansky defined the biological species as "the largest and most inclusive ... reproductive community of sexual and cross-fertilizing individuals which share in a common gene pool."[5] In a recent book he gives this definition: "A biological species is an inclusive Mendelian population; it is integrated by the bonds of sexual reproduction and parentage."[6] Grant defined the species as follows: "The sum total of the races that interbreed frequently or occasionally with one another, and that intergrade more or less continuously in their phenotypic characters, is the (biological) species."[7]

A great deal of time and labor would be needed to study sufficiently even a small portion of the sexual forms in the world to learn their crossability. Nevertheless the recognition of this type of species marks a great advance. The creationist welcomes the recognition of these units in nature on the part of evolutionists, because it marks a forward step toward agreement as to what constitutes the real unit in the living world. The concept of the creationist regarding Genesis kinds, and of the evolutionist regarding the biological species, agree delightfully on a number of points. Both agree that the species is a self-reproducing and reproductively isolated population consisting of individuals which may vary considerably among themselves in their form, structure, coloration, and body covering.

Of course not all creationists hold the same opinion with regard to the reproductive behavior of the Genesis kinds. Creationists are bound together in the doctrine that Genesis is a book inspired of God. However on subjective points they may diverge considerably. One of these points is this very matter of the crossability of the Genesis kinds. The situation is quite similar to that among evolutionists who at the Darwin Centennial in Chicago in 1959 appeared to be united in acceptance of the synthetic theory of organic evolution (that evolution is a two-stage phenomenon: the production of variation, and the sorting of the variants by natural selection). However, when it comes to discrete natural groups in nature, the groups often disagree.

Although creationist scientific literature has burgeoned in the last two decades, we cannot even guess how many creationists believe that Genesis kinds are separated from one another by reproductive gaps. Nor do we know how many think that Genesis kinds were once interfertile, but not now; or that we have no way of knowing their mutual reproductive behavior; or that we may not even be able to recognize the originally created kinds today, not to mention their reproductive behavior.

Creationists who believe that Genesis portrays the created kinds as reproductively isolated from one another reject the suggestion that kinds may have been able to hybridize in antediluvian times. They take this position because they believe that an original kind which brought forth only "after its own kind" could not hybridize with another kind. If such were to occur, then neither partner would be bringing forth after its kind. The assumed hybrid would be like neither of the parental types. Discussions of this problem involve much that is heavily speculative.

As students of origins, we remind ourselves that we are trying to get a clear understanding of the widespread biological process called microevolution, and of the assumed process called macroevolution, ie, "evolution." A differentiation of these two processes, whether real or assumed, unfortunately involves an understanding of what is meant by the vague term "species." We previously referred to what may be called "splitter" species, "lumper" species, and reputable-taxonomist species; in this chapter we are trying to understand the increasingly popular (among biologists) biological species (and the polytypic species) and how they relate to the creationist concept of the Genesis kind.

We have referred to the polytypic species above by reference to its component parts, the geographical races. The evolutionist German taxonomist O. Kleinschmidt, in 1900, was perhaps the first to comment on the difference between what Linnaeus called a species (as, for example, his assignment of separate species names to the American and the European bison) and the polytypic species that was well recognized at the close of the 1800s. Kleinschmidt believed that the polytypic species was a higher category in nature because it was commonly formed by the combination of many local species. For that reason he thought it should be given some other name than species. He suggested calling this large natural unit a *Formenkreis*. Some thirty years later in Germany, Rensch suggested that a more accurate name for the polytypic species would be *Rassenkreis*. However, though this suggestion found few adherents, the recognition of this higher category among plants and animals marked a definite advance among field biologists. A more harmonious way in taxonomy of handling the *Formenkreis* or the *Rassenkreis* was suggested by Huxley[8] in 1940 and has been almost universally adopted. He suggested that the terms *monotypic species* (a species not divided into subspecies) and *polytypic species* (a species which contains two or more subspecies) be used to distinguish between nondimensional and multidimensional populations.

Examples in North America of polytypic species among larger mammals would be (1) the red fox, *Vulpes fulva*, with its twelve subspecies distributed from Vancouver Island on the west to Newfoundland on the east, and (2) the coyote, *Canis latrans*, with its nineteen subspecies more or less isolated from one another in the western parts of the United States and Canada. However, according to Hall and Kelson[9], the greatest examples of subspeciation known in mammals are found among the small hairy animals of western United States. The southern pocket gopher, *Thomomys umbrinus* leads the list with 214 subspecies, and the northern pocket gopher, *T. talpoides*, ranks second with 66 subspecies. This high degree of subspeciation largely results from the isolation of groups because of the extreme lack of movement in the pocket gophers. The deer mouse, *Peromyscus maniculatus*, with its 66 subspecies ranges widely over the United States, and groups achieve isolation because they are so widely scattered geographically.

In the light of the components of polytypic species as presently listed, the creationist's point of view does not permit him to accept every polytypic species as the possible surviving descendants of an original Genesis kind. To illustrate, the wolves and the coyotes are listed as belonging respectively to the gray wolf (*Canis lupus*) polytypic species, and to the coyote (*Canis latrans*) polytypic species. Most creationists consider all dogs (at least wolves, coyotes, jackals, dingos, and domestic dogs) as having descended from a single created kind.

Again, as noted above, Hall and Kelson place the southern and northern pocket gophers (*Thomomys*) in separate polytypic species. Because of the general crossability and morphological similarity of all pocket gophers, eight genera and about thirty species ranging over North America (and nowhere else), creationists hold it possible that all pocket gophers have descended from a single Genesis kind whose population increased, divided, and some individuals emigrated into new areas, with each new population experiencing limited variation through the effects of microevolution.

In the creationist's opinion single polytypic species could include all living descendants of created kinds. There are numerous cases to select from among this kind of species, a fact indicated in the following statements by Ernst Mayr: (1) "It is now well established that the occurrence of polytypic species is a universal phenomenon in the animal kingdom. There is no known tribe or family in which polytypic species have not been found when looked for."[10] (2) "Most species of plants, unless highly localized, show some geographic variation, and this variation is frequently sufficient to justify nomenclatural recognition of local races. The frequency of polytypic species among plants is sometimes overlooked since it is overshadowed by more conspicuous forms of variation, such as those caused by polyploidy, apomixis, and hybridization."[11]

The song sparrow, *Passerella melodia,* is an example of a polytypic species which, from the creationist point of view, may include all living descendants of an original kind. Pioneer ornithologists in eastern North America recorded four similar groups of sparrows to which the species names, fox, *Passerella iliaca;* swamp, *P. georgiana;* lincoln, *P. lincolni;* and song, *P. melodia,* were assigned. During the exploration of the West in the middle 1800s, several additional forms of *Passerella* were discovered and different species names assigned to them. However, continued exploration revealed additional populations intermediate between all these species. As a result, all "species" were finally reduced in rank to subspecies and combined into a single polytypic species, the song sparrow, *Passerella melodia,* with more than thirty subspecies. To the creationist these song sparrows may constitute at least a portion of the living descendants of an original song-sparrow kind.

Although the true cattle of the world, genus *Bos,* are presently assigned to the species *taurus, indicus, grunniens, gaurus, frontalis, banteng,* and *sauveli;* the African buffalo to the genus and species *Syncerus caffer;* and the American and European bison to the genus *Bison* and to the species *bison* and *bonasus,* it would appear, from their crossability and similar basic morphology, that they actually constitute a single polytypic species. To the creationist they may all have descended from a single created cattle kind.

Evolutionists have increasingly acknowledged among living things a concrete entity of a higher category than they previously had recognized. Mayr comments on the effect of this: "As the new polytypic species concept began to assert itself, a certain pessimism [among evolutionists] seemed to be associated with it. It seemed as if each of the polytypic species (*Rassenkreis*) was as clearcut and as separated from other species by bridgeless gaps as if it had come into being by a separate act of creation. And this is exactly the conclusion drawn by men like Kleinschmidt and Goldschmidt. *They claim that all the evidence for intergradation between species which was quoted in the past was actually based on cases of intraspecific variation, and, in all honesty, it must be admitted that this claim is largely justified.* [Italics added.] But there is one serious flaw in the arguments of Kleinschmidt and Goldschmidt: they fail to define what *they* consider a species."[12]

Turning again to the biological species, we have noted that this category consists of a population in which all individuals are actually or potentially interfertile. That is to say, they do or can mate freely and produce fertile offspring. The genetic significance is that these individuals all draw their inheritance from a common gene pool. Perhaps we can best show the unsatisfactory nature of the biological species definition when it comes to using it in an understanding of macroevolution (interspecific variation) by citing examples from the work that has been done with vinegar flies.

Both Dobzhansky[13] and Mayr[14] speak of the races A and B of the vinegar fly, *Drosophila pseudoobscura*, which when crossed produce semisterile daughters and completely sterile sons. Dobzhansky and Epling[15] assign the new species name *D. persimilis* to race B, leaving the name *D. pseudoobscura* to apply only to race A. Although these groups are practically indistinguishable morphologically, they behave as good species biologically. The best explanation of this situation appears to be the occurrence of one or more mutations which have produced physiological differences as well as different ecological preferences.

The vinegar fly, *Drosophila*, in fact, has proved to be a genus remarkably rich in pairs and groups of morphologically similar species. To illustrate, Duda in 1925 considered the *repleta* group of *Drosophila* to contain a single species. However, Patterson, Wheeler, and Mainland have since been able to distinguish twenty-eight species in this group.[16] Duda had made his classification from museum material entirely. The multiplicity of species of this kind was revealed later through breeding experiments. In other words, the one morphological species of Duda was found to contain a number of physiological (biological) species.

Again, in his article on two species of this group, *Drosophila equinoxialis* and *D. willistoni,* Dobzhansky reports concerning their similarity of appearance, that "the differences are, however, so small that single individuals of the two species cannot be distinguished by inspection not only in museum material but even in living flies."[17] Concerning the breeding behavior between these two biological species, he says, "The reproductive isolation between them is complete."[18]

These vinegar fly studies reveal at least two clear facts: (a) The population of the biological species of the evolutionist may actually be a very different kind of population from that of the Genesis kind of the creationist and can be sorted from other biological species only in the breeding pen; and (b) the Genesis-kind category is more widely usable in that members of a kind are generally similar one to another morphologically so can be distinguished both in the living world and in the museum without recourse to the breeding pen. The biological species to the evolutionist is first and last physiological, while the created kind of the creationist is commonly first morphological but lastly and more decisively physiological. The evolutionist quite frequently will not be able to distinguish his biological species in the museum. However, by morphological details the creationist can sort out the Genesis kinds quite well in the museum from among many dead specimens, and also in the field morphologically and physiologically while the organism is going about its business of living.

As we make these assertions about what creationists believe the Genesis kinds to be, we must remember that at present there is a lack of agreement among creationists with regard to the status of the original created kinds in nature today. Actually little interest has been manifested among creationists on this point. In classification they have for convenience merely used the taxonomic lists prepared largely by evolutionists; if the subject comes up, they may speculate mildly about whether the present-day genus, or possibly family or some other category, is the created kind as it appears in our time.

Back in 1941 I accepted Linnaeus's opinion that the Genesis kind was a population of individuals who could interbreed and produce other individuals like themselves. Then I made a study of hybridization across categories in our taxonomic system. On the assumption of crossability, in the case of man, *Homo sapiens*, the species would be the created unit. In other cases we find that the dog, *Canis familiaris*, will cross with the gray wolf, *Canis lupus*; the horse, *Equus caballus*, will cross with the ass, *Equus asinus*. Here the genus would be the created unit. Again the domestic goat, genus *Capra*, will cross with the domestic sheep, genus *Ovis*, to the extent of producing fetuses which will live until just before the time for birth. A more successful generic hybrid is the case of the genus *Bison* which will cross with the domestic cow, genus *Bos*, possibly making the family the created unit.[19]. Yet again the domestic hen, family *Phasionidae*, has been crossed with the turkey, family *Meleagrididae*.[20] Thus the order would possibly become the created unit.

Before proceeding farther, we should again consider

SPECIES AND THE GENESIS KIND

Dobzhansky's differentiation between microevolution and macroevolution. Dobzhansky said that microevolution includes changes observable within the span of a human lifetime, while macroevolution is observed only on a geological scale. In his opinion, then, "macroevolution" should be used when referring to the assumption of origin of new basic kinds of organisms. Confusion over the meaning of the term macroevolution appears here because in hybridization between genera (interspecific), new species (often biological) and even genera may result. An example here would be the crossing of the radish, *Raphanus sativus,* with the cabbage, *Brassica oleracea,* with the production of a new biological genus presently called *Raphanobrassica.* In this case a new genus appeared in much less than geologic time. Thus confusion arises. Obviously "macroevolution" needs a more careful and specific definition.

What is the position of the creationist in the matter of microevolution and the crossing of species? Many species on our taxonomic lists are actually no more than subspecies of a single species at the most. We have already noticed that of true cattle, for example, seven species are now listed. These species are quite freely cross-fertile and should taxonomically be grouped into one polytypic species. Although the bison are quite freely crossable with the true cattle (genus *Bos*), still they are presently placed in the genus *Bison.* When a bison crosses with a domestic cow, a hybrid individual (the cattalo) appears which may be fertile. This suggests that the genera *Bos* and *Bison* are members of a single basic type, possibly a polytypic species. In the same manner, when a radish and a cabbage cross, they may be of the same basic type. All we need to do is to give the basic type a species name; then the *Bos-Bison* cross and the *Raphanus-Brassica* cross are actually, physiologically, intraspecific crosses, and the process could be called microevolution. In view of all demonstrable data, we may assert that no new variant has ever been known to be more than a new population within a basic type already in existence, a new population whose members are still bona fide members of the basic type to which the parents belong.

Returning now to the account of a search for the basic unit among sexual organisms, and for a name for this unit, among plants we find the same scattering of hybrid production through the various categories. Species of the same genus will commonly cross, as the bur oak with the swamp white oak.[21] Genera not infrequently cross: for example, rye with wheat, and field corn with teosinte and gamagrass. One of the most interesting crosses in plants probably is that already mentioned of radish with cabbage (plants of the genera respectively, *Raphanus* and *Brassica,* genera which stand in juxtaposition in Gray[22]), both representing genera of the mustard family. To my knowledge, among plants, members of two different families have never been crossed.

In the light of these data on crossability, and of the assumption that if organisms cross they are members of a single Genesis kind, I looked for a name for the created unit which would suggest none of the confused and arbitrary categories of present-day nomenclature. Finally I suggested (1941)[23] the name *baramin* (bārä'min, plural *baramins*), from the Hebrew roots, *bara,* created, and *min,* kind.

The boundaries of the baramin were clarified in early 1945 in response to Dobzhansky's challenge to me by letter: "You speak of a creation of basic types in a beginning; of a continuation of these kinds to the present time; and of an impossibility for these kinds to cross. Now you should either point out these kinds in nature, or keep still about them" I wanted to respond that he also had a duty—either he should point out the connecting links between his assumedly evolved kinds, or keep silent about such a thing as organic evolution ever having occurred. But I contained my native sense of unfair treatment. Feeling his challenge entirely within reason, I suggested to him the hypothesis that in final test, in every case where *true fertilization* of the egg occurs, the parents are members of the same Genesis kind (basic type).

True fertilization is necessary because in hybridization the union of the gametes may result in an embryo which does not live beyond the gastrula stage; or the fetus may die at full period; or the hybrid may be a healthy individual in every way except that it is sterile; or the hybrid may be a completely normal, fertile individual. The requirement of *true* fertilization is met when the chromosome groups of *both parents* take part in formation of the early blastomeres of the embryo. This is a distinguishing requirement for a true hybrid because offspring may be produced where the germ cells of the male take no other part in the development of a new individual than to stimulate an artificial parthenogenesis whereby the egg will proceed with its development into an embryo. In such cases the inheritance is all from the female side. The new individual is therefore not a hybrid. An example of this situation in nature is furnished by the assertion of Loeb in 1912 that practically all teleosts of the ocean would cross.[24] It is now known that in such cases the foreign sperm merely instigates development and then its nucleus is thrown out bodily in the early cleavage stages.

The reader should not confuse true fertilization of gametes with DNA hybridization. Some interesting tissue cultures are carried on in which soma (body) cells of various animals are brought together in a single culture. Some hybridization of DNA has occurred, and it has been found, for example, that different kinds of DNA from animals belonging to the same family are more similar than those from different families of the same order. When we recall that the morphology of an organism results from the peculiar chemistry of its genes, this variation in similarity of DNA is to be expected.

One of the most interesting cases of DNA hybridization occurred when human embryonic lung fibroblasts were grown in the same culture with a strain of mouse fibroblasts. In this association, in some cases, human and mouse chromosomes appeared in the same cell. However, from 75 to 95 percent of the human chromosome complement did not appear in the hybrid cells, and continued growth of the hybrid line resulted in slow elimination of *all* human chromosomes. To the creationist, such behavior in tissue cultures helps corroborate empirically the statements of Genesis which portray man and all animals originating from the same materials, the dust of the earth, at the command of one Creator. A unity within living material was a natural result. (For further details see Dobzhansky,[25] Weiss and Green,[26] and Rabovsky.[27]) A study of DNA hybridization will reveal that it is a situation quite different from that in which male and female gametes unite in true fertilization and all chromosomes of both parents proceed to build a new individual organism.

In this concept of the created kind, that of the baramin, we stress that morphological characters are important in the field and to a great extent should help distinguish one Genesis kind from another. Illustrations of this fact are so common that we often miss their significance. In the living world the baramins are usually easy to distinguish. The exception would be when a deer hunter bags a cow, or even shoots other living baramins whose misidentification is even less excusable. We look into the pasture and have no difficulty, at least at close range, in distinguishing one Genesis kind from another. Horses, cows, sheep, pigs, coyotes, jackrabbits, prairie dogs, rattlesnakes, and grass-

SPECIES AND THE GENESIS KIND 39

hoppers require of us no technical study in the breeding pen in order to discover if they are discrete entities in nature, variants of a single biological species, or possibly subspecies of a single polytypic species. Thus one advantage of the baramin is the ease with which one is distinguished from another. The Genesis kinds are the most conspicuous, discrete, and real entities in the living world.

In the early days of the evolutionists' biological-species concept, creationists hoped that the two opposing views might be drawing nearer together. The biological-species concept does in fact bring evolutionists at least a step nearer to the concept of created basic types. However, as illustrated above, in the application of the new species name *persimilis* to what was formerly race B of *Drosophila pseudoobscura,* a sharp distinction between the biological species and the baramin is brought into focus. The new species *persimilis* is described as "practically indistinguishable morphologically" from *pseudoobscura*. And again in the case of *D. equinoxialis* and *D. willistoni* the flies of the two biological species are said to be so alike in appearance as to be indistinguishable, not only in the museum but also among living specimens. Nevertheless in these four clusters of individuals four biological species are recorded because the reproductive isolation between them is either nearly or entirely complete.

From the point of view of the baramin concept, what would be the decision here? Because all four clusters of these flies are morphologically still vinegar flies, they would still be categorized as members of a single Genesis kind. The creationist recognizes that within many baramins since the beginning one or more mutations have occurred which, chemically or mechanically, make the members of a group sterile with those of another group. Still the morphological changes have never been so great as to result in a new basic type of organism. All laboratory proof confirms this. Of all the biological species which may develop within the vast vinear fly population, in not one case has it been questioned that every individual fly of whatever "species" is still a vinegar fly.

It appears that evolutionists, in their search for real entities in the living world, invariably fix their attention at too low a level. Instead of being distracted by the trees (biological species among individual vinegar flies) they need to take a few steps backward and behold the entire forest (the vinegar fly basic type or baramin).

As we mentioned before, the term *macroevolution* is poorly and inaccurately defined. We have noted that Goldschmidt used the term "for the evolution of good species and all the higher taxonomic categories."[28] Webster's Dictionary says that macroevolution is "evolutionary change involving relatively large and complex steps (as transformation of one species to another)."

In increasing numbers, evolutionists agree that biological species are "good species." They believe *Drosophila persimilis* is a good species that has developed from or within a population of the good species *D. pseudoobscura*. So we have a syllogism:
1. The development of a new good species from another good species constitutes organic evolution.
2. The good species *Drosophila persimilis* developed from the good species *D. pseudoobscura*.
3. Therefore, the development of *D. persimilis* demonstrates organic evolution.

But is this a proper syllogism? We cannot escape the fact that all vinegar flies are the same basic type of animal. Therefore, how can we escape the fact that the development of a new biological species does not necessarily constitute macroevolution, that is, organic evolution? To the

SPECIES AND THE GENESIS KIND   41

creationist this reproductive isolation of a cluster of vinegar flies at the most accomplishes no more than the appearance of a new population of vinegar fly, ie, *microevolution*. The student must think his way through this carefully, or he will end up in a state of confusion along with so many others to whom microevolution and macroevolution are entangled in a jumble of definitions.

The basic types, the created kinds, the baramins, stand so manifest and so clearly defined in nature by appearance and reproductive behavior as to constitute a delight to the student observant enough to fix his attention upon the level of the forest rather than upon the trees which constitute it. Very detailed work in science must be done with the trees, but basic and sweeping generalizations among living things require a wider look at a higher level.

CHAPTER 4

The Physical Basis of Heredity

As we have seen, basic types, although they may vary considerably, continue to survive from generation to generation. As the creationist sees it, this succession of generations of all living forms has gone on for thousands of years, while the evolutionist would place the origin of crustaceans, echinoderms, arrowworms, and mollusks in the Cambrian period which he dates as 500 to 600 million years ago.

Note that by the very same characteristics by which we distinguish a mollusk from a starfish today, we distinguish them among the fossils of the Cambrian period. So we conclude that the hereditary process by which a starfish is still undisputably a starfish today, must indeed be a reliable, dependable, constant method. We set hen eggs beneath a patient hen and never doubt that we will get chicks, never ducklings. To keep the milk supply coming we breed the high-producing family cow to a good bull. Would we not be flabbergasted if she should bring forth a colt instead of a calf? The fact that basic kinds still bring forth after their kinds is so common a phenomenon that we often fail to ponder its significance.

Let us set any one of the more complex animals before us. Where in the organism does the hereditary mechanism reside—the factor that makes each succeeding generation so like the preceding one that there is no question as to the

THE PHYSICAL BASIS OF HEREDITY 43

offspring of a dog also being a dog? We are aware that each organism is made up of organs with their specific work to do in some such system as the skeletal, the muscular, the nervous, the circulatory, the respiratory, the digestive, the hormonal, and so on. We are aware that each organ is made up of different tissues—nerve, muscular, connective, epithelial, and others.

It is when we come to the components of the tissues, the cells, that we find the genes, the hereditary material. Specifically, the genes are located in the nucleus of the cell. The hereditary material is marshaled along the long axis of each chromosome. In each body-cell nucleus the chromosomes occur in pairs, one member having come from each parent. The number of pairs varies in body cells from two in the parasitic worm *Ascaris* up to 100 in crayfish and even higher numbers of pairs in some ferns and protozoans.

The chromosome number in mature germ cells is called haploid, and that in body cells diploid. Some diploid numbers in animals are as follows: man 46, Rhesus monkey 48, horse 66, cattle 60, cat 38, dog 78, rat 42, mouse 40, chicken 77 and 78, goldfish 94, housefly 12, vinegar fly 8, mosquito 6, honeybee female 32. Diploid numbers of a few plants are as follows: cabbage 18, radish 18, bean 22, tobacco 48, onion 16, corn 20, bread wheat 42, upland cotton 52, apple 34 and 51, orange 18 and 27 and 36, yellow pine 24, scarlet oak 24.[1] Considering all the chromosomes as a set in each cell, they constitute its chromosome complement.

Within each organism, then, are organs; within organs, tissues; within the tissues, cells; within each cell, a nucleus; within each nucleus, a set of chromosomes; within each chromosome, a linear arrangement of *genes*. Each gene has specific chemical and physical properties that determine the nature of the phenotype (what we perceive with our senses). Amazingly, these minute molecules, the genes, are the centers from which radiate the chemical influences that find their way throughout the body. These influences direct the expression of the different characters which distinguish a man from an ape, a mouse from an elephant, a dwarf apple from a giant redwood. Each of the body cells has its chromosome complement containing the host of genes which set the pattern of all things hereditary in that organism. The material of which each gene is composed has the ability to replicate (reproduce) itself *exactly,* and only rarely does this reproduction lead to a gene with properties different from that of the original. In this exact replication is based the fact of the continuity of the gene complement (genotype) from one generation to the next.

A chemical analysis of an organism shows that thirty-five chemical elements are relatively common. The six most common are carbon, hydrogen, oxygen, nitrogen, phosphorus, and sulfur. In living creatures the elements arrange themselves into different classes of molecules such as fats, carbohydrates, lipids, vitamins, amino acids, purines, and pyrimidines. Many of the smaller molecules are in turn formed into larger units called *macromolecules.* Proteins are macromolecules, consisting of long chains of amino acids. Such molecules may contain thousands of atoms.

Proteins form the structure of skin, hair, and cartilage; many of them act as enzymes in catalyzing biochemical reactions. In addition to the large protein molecules is another class of macromolecules called nucleic acids, formed of a five-carbon sugar (either deoxyribose or ribose), phosphorus, and nitrogen-containing molecules known as purines and pyrimidines. The two kinds of nucleic acids differ. One of them is called *deoxyribonucleic acid* (DNA), and the other *ribonucleic acid* (RNA). In DNA the five-carbon sugar is *deoxyribose;* its purines are adenine and guanine;

THE PHYSICAL BASIS OF HEREDITY

its pyrimidines are thymine and cytosine. The five-carbon sugar of RNA is *ribose;* although its purines and one of its pyrimidines, cytosine, are as in DNA, its second pyrimidine is uracil instead of thymine. Structurally, DNA is double-stranded (except in some viruses) while RNA is single-stranded. (For further information see more detailed expositions, for instance, Loewy and Siekevitz.[2])

The units which make up DNA and RNA are generally similar in all animals and all plants. To the creationist this similarity of genetic material is a most impressive demonstration of the unity of living things, a unity resulting from their origin from a single source—the "dust [elements] of the earth"—at the command of one Creator.

The number of genes in different creatures is puzzling. Says Dobzhansky, "The diversity of living beings is evidently based not on the proportions but on the arrangements of the genetic 'letters.' The amounts of DNA per cell are, as a rule, uniform in different tissues and individuals of the same species. Sex cells carry one-half as much DNA as do body cells. The amounts vary, however, in different organisms. . . . More complex organisms generally have more DNA per cell than do simpler ones, but this rule has conspicuous exceptions. Man is far from the top of the list, being exceeded by *Amphiuma* [an apode amphibian], *Protopterus* [a lungfish], and even ordinary frogs and toads. Why this should be so has long been a puzzle. It seems unreasonable that Amphiuma needs twenty-six times as many genes as man does."[3]

Molecular biologists agree that the genetic material in both higher and lower organisms is DNA (or RNA in certain viruses). Experiments have demonstrated in different organisms that, although proteins and carbohydrates, for example, undergo continual breakdown and resynthesis in cellular metabolism, DNA does not. Measurements of the amount of DNA in each cell of a given organism show that it remains essentially constant, while the amounts of other cell constituents vary from one type of cell to another. Thus DNA apparently possesses within itself two required characteristics of the hereditary material: (1) It is transmitted unchanged from generation to generation; and (2) it is not metabolized.

Taylor[4] gives a brief story of DNA. Over a period reaching up to the middle 1900s, the names of various scientists appear—Miescher, Hoppe-Seyler, Tswett, Martin, Synge, Chargaff, Davidson, Wilkins, Franklin, Pauling, Corey, Crick, Watson, Stahl, and Meselson. Wilkins, Franklin, and co-workers discovered important physical characteristics of DNA. Francis Crick and James Watson used their information, combined it with more up-to-date facts, and then proposed that DNA consisted of a double spiral, with the bases on the inside, opposed in pairs, and linked by the weak interatomic force known as a hydrogen bond. Thus we see DNA (the gene) as two coiled polynucleotide chains bound together crosswise by hydrogen bonding between a purine (adenine or guanine) and a pyrimidine (cytosine or thymine). The restriction in pairing of nucleotides is accomplished by the mechanical limitation of the H bonding of adenine to thymine and of guanine to cytosine. This would account for the conservation of the genetic material. Thus if the order of nucleotides along one polynucleotide chain is A G T C A C, the sequence along the other chain must be the complementary sequence of T C A G T G.

Crick and Watson describe the duplication of DNA: "Now our model for deoxyribonucleic acid is, in effect, a *pair* of templates, each of which is complementary to the other. We imagine that prior to duplication the hydrogen bonds are broken, and the two chains unwind and separate. Each chain then acts as a template for the formation onto itself of

THE PHYSICAL BASIS OF HEREDITY

a new companion chain, so that eventually we shall have *two* pairs of chains, where we only had one before. Moreover, the sequence of the pairs of bases will have been duplicated exactly."[5]

As the infinitely complex process is presently understood, DNA (each gene) probably remains in the nucleus during the life of the cell. There it has two functions: First, it serves as a template for its own replication before cell division (described in the words of Watson and Crick above); second, it serves as a template for the synthesis of messenger RNA (m-RNA). In this second function there must first be a breaking of the H bonds in the DNA and a separation of its two polynucleotide chains as occurred in its own reproduction. According to Levine[6] only one strand of the DNA molecule serves as a template in the synthesis of m-RNA. This messenger is synthesized upon the DNA template from nucleotides in the nucleus. Messenger RNA then passes out of the nucleus into the cytoplasm where (to oversimplify a complicated process) it takes its place upon the surface of a ribosome and proceeds to synthesize from the cytoplasmic amino acids one of the specific proteins which make any plant or animal a bona fide member of its original basic type.

Thus it has been said that the functional genetic unit, the gene, has as its sole task the accomplishment of the synthesis of a single specific protein. However, increasing evidence indicates that certain genes never yield proteins. Examples are the genes for the transfer of ribosomal RNA. Then another important class of RNA remains confined to the nucleus, apparently involved in gene regulation, which may also fall into this category.

Commenting on the assumed specificity of gene action, Dobzhansky says: "A hypothesis once widely accepted among geneticists postulated that each gene is responsible for the production of one and only one enzyme. This one-gene-one-enzyme hypothesis is now modified to state that each structural gene is transcribed into a single RNA, and the latter is translated into a single polypeptide chain of a protein. It by no means follows that every gene produces just a single character or trait. This is a misconception refuted by the striking manifold (pleiotropic) effects of many genes."[7] Together the genes of complex organisms accomplish, in the development of the organism from fertilized egg to adult, those peculiar characteristics which make the differences between a horse and a dog, between corn and beans.

With regard to the significance of such a physical basis for heredity, Levine says: "DNA is the source of *genetic information* necessary for the development of phenotypes. Every organism possesses a vast array of hereditary characteristics, and these in turn reflect many different kinds of genetic information. Diversity of genetic information is found in DNA as the only letters in an alphabet for a code or language that depends upon the sequence and perhaps the ratio of pairs of A-T and G-C nucleotides. A DNA molecule may contain 10^7 pairs of nucleotides. If we assume that half of the pairs are A-T and half are G-C, the number of different sequences of pairs possible is immense."[8]

As we review this basic mechanism of inheritance, it is almost an overwhelming concept that in the different arrangements of only two pairs (the same two pairs) of nucleotides in a linear series in each of a cluster of chromosomes lie the determiners for the setting of the stage which shall produce a man or a mouse. The simplicity with complexity in the plan is amazing, and it appears most impossible that chance alone could ever have wrought so perfect a system for a production of like from like. The handiwork of a Supreme Being, an Honest Workman, stands revealed. As sincere scientists in a natural world, we endeavor to think His thoughts after Him.

CHAPTER 5

Causes of Variation in Organisms

In our study of the problem of origins we need to acquaint ourselves with the processes of change which may operate in living things so that we can determine their quality and magnitude. Of course we know that variation does occur in plants and animals. This fact becomes obvious as we compare the differences in appearance between a Nordic and a Hottentot, a Percheron and a Shetland pony, a great Dane and a toy poodle, dent field corn and popcorn, Better Times and a wild rose. What mechanisms operate to produce this variation? Is there any limit to how far the changes can go?

Bearing in mind the basic mechanism of heredity outlined briefly in the preceding chapter, let us now review causes of change which occur in organisms, endeavoring to discover how the basic types of plants and animals may have appeared upon our earth. Variations among living things may be divided into two large classes: nonhereditary (environmental, nongenetic), and hereditary (genetic).

The nonhereditary variations are not caused by genetic differences but by environment, including variations produced by differential feeding, humidity, light, temperature, training, and so on. An example would be the contrast in appearance of a stunted spruce tree growing at timberline and a fine specimen growing at a lower level. Again, a human being exposed to much sunshine may develop a deep coat of tan. The ability to produce melanin pigment varies from the person who can develop a heavy layer of the pigment to an albino who can develop none. However, the heavily tanned person knows that his color soon fades when his skin is shaded from the direct light. Even in generations of suntanned ancestors, the acquired tan is purely environmental, not inherited.

Let us recall that the phenotype (exterior appearance) of any organism is necessarily a result of the interaction of a genotype (genes present) with an environment; both are necessary. Some genes of the genotype of an organism may never, even though dominant, manifest themselves unless they experience just the right environment. To illustrate, sun-red corn may live from generation to generation as a yellow-seeded corn so long as, during growth, the husk shades the ear during the milk stage of its seeds. One must strip down the husk and let the direct sunlight fall on the seeds while in the milk in order to get the photochemical reaction which produces red pigment in the seeds. This same situation holds, more or less, for all factors in the genotype. The genotype sets the stage, but afterward what actually takes place on the stage depends on the fitness of the environment.

As an illustration of genotypic influence vs. environmental, breeders of agricultural plants look for even slight genotypic improvements in yield and quality, since they may be expected to recur again and again in the progeny of the improved variety. However, yields are influenced not only by genotype but also by environmental factors such as the quality of the soil, the amount of soil moisture, heat, light, and the quantity of the fertilizer. Obviously one must know whether a difference in yield between several samples of seed is predominantly genotypic or environmental. Experiments are devised whereby the relative influence of

CAUSES OF VARIATION IN ORGANISMS

genotypic and environmental factors can be determined.

Turning to hereditary variations, changes with which the student of origins is most concerned, we note that these may come about in various ways. Let us summarize them as (1) recombinations, (2) gene mutations, and (3) chromosomal aberrations, sometimes called chromosomal mutations.

1. *Recombinations.* As the term suggests, genes already present in certain combinations may through the process of reduction division (separation during the development of germ cells of each member of a chromosome pair into different daughter cells), and then through the process of fertilization, be united in new combinations, producing new characters. One example of a recombination is the birth of a red-and-white calf to a Holstein line which has been only black-and-white for a number of generations. Other examples are the appearance of walnut comb on a fowl with single and rose-combed parents and the production of gray rats by crossing a black parent with a yellow one. These effects are reversions or "throwbacks" and are not new differences. Although they constitute the commonest source of differently appearing individuals, still they can give rise to nothing really new. They come from arrangements of genetic elements already in existence; without doubt they have already appeared many times in the history of the animal or plant.

2. *Gene mutations.* A gene mutation is a heritable alteration in a single gene. As we have seen, in the complicated double helix of chemical substances, there is considerable room in which a mutation could occur. A gene mutation implies that the genetic material can undergo some sort of change that results in the production of an altered phenotype. According to Levine, "Gene mutations represent changes that have occurred at the level of one to a few

nucleotides within the DNA molecule and below the resolution of the electron microscope."[1] According to Dobzhansky, "Most [gene] mutations are caused by substitution of a single amino acid in a protein, and of a single nucleotide in the DNA chain coding this protein."[2]

As a rule genes are so stable that the natural mutation rate is very low. Many species have remained much the same for thousands of years. The brachiopods among animals, and seaweeds and *Ginkgo* among plants, are examples of organisms in which almost no changes are observed in present-day species as compared with fossils. The comparative rarity of such changes is a fortunate thing, because gross mutations are usually harmful to the organism, and the majority of mutations threaten the organism's survival. This is to be expected as we remember that the organism is a delicately adjusted mechanism, and a random change would more likely be injurious than beneficial.

There are three kinds of gene mutations: visible, biochemical, and lethal.

In *visible* mutations the phenotypic effects alter the organism's morphology. These visible mutations in the fruit fly may be either dominant, as bar eye, or recessive, as white eye. Other visible mutations are the short-legged or Ancon breed of sheep; albino man and albino animals such as rabbits, rats, mice, guinea pigs, foxes, skunks, squirrels, and birds; hornless cattle; double-eared cattle; pacing horses; many-toed cats; mule-footed swine; and bulldog-faced dogs.

Conspicuous gene mutations of the visible class in plants include the Shirley poppy, remarkable for its wide range of colors, which originated from a single plant of a small red poppy common in English cornfields; double petunias, roses, azaleas, stocks, carnations, daisies, and other plant clusters which arose from single-flowered plants; dwarf portulaca; striped sugar cane; blotched leaf in corn; the Boston fern; red sunflowers; red sweet potatoes; spineless cacti; and the Concord grape.

A second class of gene mutations may be called *biochemical*. They represent a loss of a specific biochemical function, since the mutant organism no longer has the ability to synthetize an essential metabolite such as an amino acid or a vitamin. Or this kind of mutation may be the cause of the loss of an organism's ability to make a specific protein, most often an enzyme necessary for the normal function of some essential process. Possibly such a loss or change is the underlying cause of most mutations. In such a situation, of course, the biochemical mutation would cause death unless the organism is otherwise supplied with the metabolite it cannot synthesize.

Lethal mutations. These chemical changes appear early in development and cause the death of the organism in the embryonic stage.

Can mutations create new species? Biologists do not agree. Dobzhansky says: "Most biologists were skeptical, and justifiably so, of the mutation theory of de Vries, who claimed that new species arise by sudden mutations. Likewise, when Morgan and his associates described mutant *Drosophilae,* many biologists remained skeptical, because these mutants looked like a collection of freaks rather than changes fit to serve as raw materials of evolution. Some biologists continue, though no longer justifiably, to be skeptical. The reason is that most mutations, large as well as small, are more or less deleterious to their carriers. Mutation appears to be a destructive, rather than a constructive, process. One should not forget, however, that a mutation is neither useful nor harmful in the abstract; it can be so only in some environment. If the environment is not specified, the statement that a mutation is useful or harmful is meaningless. A mutant that is harmful when its carrier is placed in one environment may be neutral in another, and useful in still other environments. Furthermore, a mutant gene does not exert its effects on adaptedness regardless of what other genes an individual carries; a changed gene may be harmful on some genetic backgrounds but useful on others."[3]

3. *Chromosomal aberrations (chromosomal mutations).* Composing this type of change there are two major classes: (a) changes in chromosome number (ploidy), and (b) changes in the chromosome structure that result in alterations of gene order or number.

Three kinds of ploidy are recognized: *haploidy,* where the chromosome complement contains only a single member of each normal chromosome pair; *polyploidy,* where each chromosome complement contains more than two entire individuals of each chromosome; and *heteroploidy,* where a chromosome is subtracted from or added to the normal set. The situation in which a pair of each of the chromosomes is present is diploidy, and is considered to be the normal arrangement.

How many chromosomes do different organisms have? The chromosome count of radiolarians (one-celled marine animals) runs to several hundred. As many as 208 are found in each cell of the crayfish *Cambarus immunis.* In a large sample of 2413 species of plants, over one half had less than twelve chromosomes as a haploid number. Twelve chromosomes in the haploid set was the modal point where 391 species out of the 2413 were grouped. Eight in the 2413 had the same number as man, 23 in each haploid set.[4] The correlation between chromosome number and gene number is very low, longer chromosomes commonly having many more genes than shorter ones. We might add that identity in chromosome number does not necessarily have any relation to the crossability. Some of the creatures hav-

CAUSES OF VARIATION IN ORGANISMS

ing the same chromosome number as man (diploid 46) are: marmoset monkey, meadow mouse, shelduck (*Tadorna*), water snake, worm lizard, six-lined racerunner (lizard), an Old World lizard, and four bony fishes.[5]

Returning now to the haploids, these individuals occur normally in the reproduction of such animals as bees, wasps, certain moths, and rotifers in which unfertilized eggs develop into males. In some animals, eg, starfish, frogs, salamanders, and rabbits, the eggs may be induced artificially to develop into haploid individuals. Often in such cases the diploid number is restored through a division of chromosomes not accompanied by cellular division. Haploids have been found in several plant species, for example, Jimson weed, tobacco, tomato, and wheat. Such individuals may be induced by cold, radiation, or other external changes. But because of their rarity and infertility these forms probably play little part in adding to the supply of new natural variants.

The second kind of ploidy, *polyploidy*, appears to be more important. A number of leading evolutionist geneticists hold that this process of variation is the most promising in the matter of generation of new species. Two types of polyploids are recognized: *autopolyploids*, where there has been a multiplication of the basic chromosome number characteristic of a *single* race; and *allopolyploids*, where the individuals have arisen from a fusion of gametes having more than the reduced or haploid number, but which have come from *different* races, species, or genera.

Autopolyploidy may occur spontaneously in nature or may arise from adventitious buds arising at grafts or after decapitation in tomato and nightshade plants. Some of the shoots which develop from these buds in callus tissue formed at the cut surface are polyploid. Flowers on these shoots may perpetuate the condition through sexual reproduction. Treatment of buds and seeds with the alkaloid colchicine from the autumn crocus is a simple way of inducing polyploidy experimentally. Under the influence of this alkaloid, splitting of chromosomes occurs, but the cell fails to form two daughter cells at the time, thus doubling the chromosome number.

Of particular interest to us is the fact that autopolyploids may possibly occur naturally in the field. Muntzing[6] lists fifty-eight such apparent examples in Europe. Some very intriguing cases in our country among species of spiderworts *(Tradescantia)* are described by Anderson and Sax.[7] *T. occidentalis* is distributed over the prairie states from the Rocky Mountains east to the Mississippi River. Plants having twice the normal number of chromosomes (tetraploids) are found over most of this area. The range of *T. canaliculata* lies mostly east of that of the former species, and its individuals are also largely tetraploids. However, there is a fairly broad strip just west of the Mississippi in which both species are largely diploid. According to Anderson, the ancestral native soil for these species was an area in this strip where diploid forms of both species grow. Tetraploids developed in this area and spread outward, *T. canaliculata* going chiefly east and northeast, while *T. occidentalis* spread to the north and northwest. The thought is that the tetraploid races were better adapted to those environments than the diploid races.

It would appear that the systemic effect of polyploidy is similar to that of mutation. Any change from the normal condition which might be produced by polyploidy could be favorable for the organism under some environmental conditions and unfavorable under others. However, since either addition or loss of chromosomes, possibly through disturbance of the normal finely adjusted balance among the genes which achieves the amazing phenomenon of each

CAUSES OF VARIATION IN ORGANISMS

living thing, usually lessens the vitality of the offspring, the reproductive powers of the new individuals would more frequently be impaired. This would be a limiting factor in the usefulness of ploidy in the production of variation.

Some interesting allopolyploids have been produced in the laboratory. One of particular interest has already been mentioned—the intergeneric hybrid between radish, *Raphanus sativus*, and cabbage, *Brassica oleracea*, made by Karpechenko. Both parents have nine pairs of chromosomes, and individuals of the first hybrid generation have eighteen univalents. The individuals of the first hybrid generation are nearly sterile; most plants produce no seeds at all, but some do produce a few. These seeds from this generation give rise to individuals with thirty-six chromosomes in each cell (tetraploid). These plants are irregularly fertile. Unfortunately, this hybrid has a root like the cabbage and a top like the radish. This feeble and variable plant, which must be pampered in order for it to continue, has been named *Raphanobrassica*, a fusion of the generic names of the radish and the cabbage.

The production of allopolyploids in the laboratory reveals a mechanism in nature which *may* have functioned to some limited extent in producing complexity within original kinds. However, these forms usually show such great irregularities in the distribution of their chromosomes, accompanied with prevalent infertility, that they very likely would not be able to compete successfully in nature and thereby survive. Thus a laboratory demonstration of the effectiveness of ploidy in the production of new species is still largely lacking. The evidence for the service of ploidy in producing variation still remains chiefly of the subjective type.

Numerous examples of plant species appear to be cases of allopolyploidy. The origin of the marsh grass *Spartina townsendii*, as suggested by Huskins,[8] apparently illustrates such a case. This species was discovered occupying a single locality in southern England in 1870. A rapid spread of this grass was recorded a short time later. By 1902 it occupied thousands of acres along the English coast, and in 1906 it had appeared on the coast of France. Because of its desirable agricultural properties it has now been introduced into many parts of the world. Systematists have decided that because of its morphological characteristics it must be a hybrid between *S. stricta*, a native European species known for three hundred years, and *S. alterniflora*, a native species of America which had been introduced into England and become common in some localities. The chromosome number of the former is twenty-eight pairs, whereas that of the latter is thirty-five pairs. This would mean that an allotetraploid of these two species would have 126 chromosomes. *S. townsendii* actually shows 126 plus or minus two. Thus it seems reasonable to assume that *S. townsendii* may have arisen as a tetraploid hybrid of the other two species. The superior adaptability of this possible hybrid is demonstrated by its overrunning both *S. stricta* and *S. alterniflora* when meeting them in natural competition.

The results of cytogenetic investigations on species of wheat (*Triticum*) and the related genus *Aegilops* (goat grass) made by Sax and Sax, Sapehin, Watkins, Bleier, and Kihara are interesting in this connection. The fifteen described species of wheat fall into three classes: viz, the *einkorn* group of three species each of which has seven pairs of chromosomes (diploid), the *emmer* group of eight species, composing the "hard" wheats, which have fourteen pairs each (tetraploid), and the *vulgare* group of four species, commonly called the "soft" wheats, each member of which has forty-two chromosomes (twenty-one pairs and hexaploid).

In this case, with few exceptions, the hybrids between

CAUSES OF VARIATION IN ORGANISMS

species with the same chromosome number are fully fertile. The hybrids between the members of the emmer and vulgare groups are pentaploid, showing fourteen bivalents and seven univalents at meiosis. Crosses of emmer and einkorn have from four to seven bivalents and from seven to thirteen univalents. The vulgare-einkorn cross produces from none to as many as ten bivalents, seven being the usual number, at least in certain crosses.

These relationships have been interpreted to mean that the einkorn, emmer, and vulgare groups have, respectively, one, two, and three sets of seven chromosomes which are different from each other. It has been thought that the species of the vulgare group are allohexaploids, their origin being due to a cross with a species of *Aegilops*. Just what the process of development has been has not yet been determined, but the case is an interesting one in that it serves as an illustration of the chromosome relations within the members of a related group. That several modern species have come from a few can be sensibly concluded. These variation changes of wheat are possibly of two kinds: species formation through new combinations of chromosome sets, and these in turn combined with gene mutations and new arrangements of genes. The very greatest apparent changes here have done no more than to erect additional species within the kind of grass involved in the crosses.

With regard to the third kind of ploidy, *heteroploidy*, it has been studied in detail in the Jimson weed (*Datura*), in the evening primrose (*Oenothera*), and in the vinegar fly (*Drosophila*). Heteroploid forms, it will be recalled, are those which differ from the normal members of the species by one or possibly two chromosomes more or less. This means that in some way at least one member of the usual diploid complement is lacking entirely or that there may be three members in a "pair" instead of two. These forms appear sporadically and show numerous and generally slight departures from the wild or normal type in many characters. Because they never breed true and are of lower fertility than normal diploids, they probably do not become established as new types in nature.

That polyploidy may be widespread among plants is indicated by an examination of the chromosome numbers of various genera. The case of species of wheat with their 7, 14, and 21 pairs has been mentioned. Some other genera with the chromosome number of included species are *Chrysanthemum*, 9, 18, 27, 36, and 45 pairs; meadow rue, 7, 14, 21, 28, 35, and 42 pairs; roses, 14, 21, 28, and 35 pairs; *Solanum* (nightshade), 12, 18, 24, 30, 48, 54, 60, and 72 pairs. Various cultivated varieties of garden flowers, vegetables, crop plants, and fruit trees appear to be polyploids. Apparent triploid and tetraploid varieties are known and cultivated among hyacinths, tulips, lilies, and others. Some varieties of these kinds of flowers were experimentally produced. Polyploidy is of considerable economic value in cultivated varieties of cotton.

Quite likely some of the "new" forms developed by Burbank in his outcrossing experiments, if examined for their chromosomal composition, would turn out to be polyploids.

The abundance of apparent polyploids in plants and their relative scarcity among animals is one of the most striking differences within the variants in the two kingdoms. About the only authentic instances of tetraploidy in animals is in brine shrimps (*Artemia*) and the nematode worm *Ascaris*. Indications of ploidy are found in a study of the chromosome numbers of flatworms, leeches, and a few other annelids, all of which are hermaphroditic (bisexual). The reason there is apparently much less polyploidy in animals than in plants may be that many higher plants are hermaphroditic, while animals are usually of two sexes dif-

CAUSES OF VARIATION IN ORGANISMS

ferentiated by the diploid mechanism of segregation and combination.

We have now discussed (1) recombinations, (2) gene mutations, and (3) chromosomal aberrations, part (a) ploidy. We now come to part (b) of chromosomal aberrations, those changes in the chromosome structure that result in alterations of gene order or number. These changes consist of deletions, duplications, translocations, and inversions. Deletions (deficiencies) and duplications appear to involve losses or multiplications of single genes or of a part of a gene, or they may affect larger regions of the chromosome so that several to many genes are modified. Therefore such changes are basically distinct from the latter two, which merely change the arrangements of the genes and not their number. Addition or subtraction of genes is usually accompanied with effects which can be seen, while translocations and inversions may not be apparent on the surface.

Illustrations of effects produced by demonstrated deficiencies are the notched wing of *Drosophila* described by Bridges and Mohr and the waltzing gait in mice explained by Gates. Mice with this deficiency in this gene complement cannot run in a straight line and usually whirl about in small circles. Study of *Drosophila* has shown that most deficiencies are lethal. According to Sturtevant and Beadle, "Duplications in *Drosophila* have phenotypic [visible] effects more or less in proportion to their lengths. Short ones may have very slight effects. Longer ones have progressively stronger effects—usually in roughening of the eyes, changes in the shape of the wings, modifications of bristles."[9]

Translocations have actually been seen in the cells of Datura (eg, Jimson weed), corn, *Drosophila*, and other organisms. Among plants in which these changes have occurred are peas, bellflower, onions, tulips, peonies, many grasses, spiderworts, and evening primroses. Very few such changes have been found in animals. In several species of seed plants wild populations may contain chromosome sets that differ from one another by reciprocal translocations. It is also clear that related species sometimes differ in this respect and that translocation has been of importance in accomplishing diversity within groups.

Genes appear to be strung along end to end in the chromosome. Thus translocations which would not be expected to break exactly between genes would suggest position effects. If genes were entirely independent in each instance, it would make no difference if their arrangement in a chromosome were 1 2 3 4 5 6 or 1 2 3 6 5 4. But owing to evident position effects, changes in the serial order of genes are important in the development of variants from a normal form. Usually no appreciable reduction of the reproductive power takes place in the individuals in which inversion has occurred. Some situations appear to indicate that in *Datura* races show circles or chains of chromosomes at meiosis (mitosis with halving of number of chromosomes) in addition to bivalents.

In concluding this brief treatment of hereditary changes in the basic mechanism of heredity, we wish to emphasize one outstanding fact. Even if it be allowed that all these known processes of variation accomplish the *greatest* changes that investigators claim for them, mutations in vinegar flies merely resulted in new variants *within* the type. No one has ever conceived of the results as being anything other than vinegar flies. Autopolyploidy in spiderwort resulted in additional variants within the spiderwort type. Allopolyploids in marsh grass were additional variants of marsh grass.

Among animals tetraploidy in roundworms and brine shrimps merely produces new variants of roundworms or of shrimps. Heteroploidy in evening primroses merely produced varieties of primroses. Deletions and duplications

CAUSES OF VARIATION IN ORGANISMS 63

merely produced waltzing mice from normal mice and notched-wing vinegar flies from normal vinegar lifes. Translocations in Jimson weed and corn merely resulted in new variants of Jimson weed and corn.

It is thought that inversions of genes within the chromosome may have been active in the development of the fruit fly genus *Drosophila*. Sinnott, Dunn, and Dobzhansky state that "pericentric inversions have been active in the evolution of this genus (*Drosophila*). Similar evidence exists for grasshoppers and, less directly, for some other animals and plants."[10]

However, if inversions have produced some of the species of the genus *Drosophila*, then, by evolutionist definition, here is a case where macroevolution has occurred. This would be true if we were to define macroevolution as "interspecific variation," ie, the production of new species. However that this cannot be accepted as a definition of macroevolution (which in current usage refers to the assumed appearance of *new basic types*, ie, organic evolution) is obvious when we recall that all the species of the genus *Drosophila* are 100 percent vinegar flies. Therefore, all inversion in vinegar flies has done is merely to produce new variants of bona fide vinegar flies. *This kind of development could never result in organic evolution.*

What, then, has been accomplished by inversion? Just this: variation within a basic type (vinegar flies), no more. And that is *microevolution*. According to all demonstrable evidence, no change greater than variants *within* a basic type has been observed. This is *microevolution,* in this instance the development of new variant flies within the vinegar fly type. The term *macroevolution* should be reserved for such speculative, assumed, and undemonstrable cases as the development of new basic types.

After all these processes have achieved their greatest

possible changes, we still have nothing newer than vinegar flies, spiderworts, radish-cabbage hybrid, marsh grass, primroses, roundworms, brine shrimps, corn, and Jimson weeds. To sum it up, nothing higher than microevolution has been achieved by all these processes of change. The crucial point lies right here: *Each of these basic kinds is set off from every other basic kind by some "residual part" which no amount of gene change can erase.*

Dobzhansky states that even between species "it must be admitted that in no case have all the differences between two good species been completely resolved into gene changes."[11] If this is true of species, what can be said of the differences which set off one group of species from another species group? If we stick to the facts, we must recognize that *no present-day natural process is capable of accomplishing the change necessary to bridge the discontinuity between kinds now so widely evident in nature.*

A study of fossil forms shows that representatives of the large systematic groups are just as complex at their "earliest" appearance in the rocks as are their descendants today. Sequoia, beech, hazelnut, cottonwood, oak, willow, linden, and elm are as distinct at their earliest appearance as fossils as are the living trees today. In some cases the *species* of these fossil ancestors are not identical to our modern *species* within each respective kind. They may be as different from our modern species as two of our modern species of the same basic kind differ from each other.

The same occurs among the animals. Credit can be given to the concept of evolution here only as it directed attention to these processes of variation. The student may assume as many millions of years since the formation of fossils as he likes, *yet all the processes of change have not accomplished, even in a single case, the erasure of the discontinuity which marks off the different kinds of organisms.*

CAUSES OF VARIATION IN ORGANISMS 65

We need not become confused by the fact that processes of change apparently have operated in some variable basic types of organisms *since their creation*. These populations produced variants to which taxonomists have assigned the terms species, genera, and even families. An example is Darwin's finches on the Galápagos Islands. David Lack [12] divides these finches into three genera (some taxonomists have assigned six and seven genera) and fourteen species. The finch populations of all the islands have been placed in the subfamily *Geospizinae,* endemic to the Galápagos, of the world family *Fringillidae* (all finches). The inadequacy of the terms microevolution and macroevolution, as defined by evolutionists, is obvious in such cases. We should remember that, while taxonomic categories are arbitrarily chosen, the individual organism is the natural reality, and these individuals are grouped naturally into morphological-physiological groups which we may call basic kinds or types (baramins). We need not argue about the variously defined "species" or debate processes of microevolution and macroevolution upon such low-level, vague, fluctuating populations. The clusters we call species may be legitimate game for taxonomists, but the high-level, enduring basic types (including many "biological" species) lie clearly before the gaze of the physiologist and for the biologist constitute the true building blocks of the living world.

The student of Darwin's finches is impressed with the similarity of all populations of these birds. In most respects, other than beak differences, the individuals of these populations are "closely similar to each other" (to use Lack's words).[13] As one studies Lack's Figure 3, page 19, showing all Darwin's finches, he is impressed that they easily could have come from one, or possibly two, lines of one basic type of bird. Although considerable change has apparently developed in the beaks of the different populations, still whatever processes of variation operated, they have done no more than produce an interesting community of finches. Is this microevolution or macroevolution? Since no new basic types have appeared, we must consider this another case of microevolution, even though taxonomists tell us that new species and even genera apparently developed.

Throughout the living world the greatest actual changes that the evolutionist has found are the mere production of additional variants *within groups already present and clearly set off in nature.* Nevertheless he is optimistic and has great faith in his theory. He commonly says, when presented with these difficulties, "Just give the processes more time" However, the thoughtful student can see that such an attitude is not reasonable, because natural laws do not change with passing millennia. If we cannot lift ourselves by our bootstraps today, we could not do it in a million years. If processes of variation today are not erasing the differences between kinds, neither could they do it in millions of years.

How does the theory of special creation fare in the light of these known causes of variation? The creationist turns to Genesis and reads that each kind of plant yields seed according to its own kind. Genesis 1:12. He next turns to nature to see what Genesis means. He sees that both plants and animals still bring forth after their respective kinds. He finds that, even with all forces of change operating at maximum strength, vinegar flies still continue to bring forth vinegar flies and corn continues to bring forth corn. He finds in the fossil record that this same discontinuity has existed since the earliest natural record; all the work of all the scientists can demonstrate only the minor differences which have come in by microevolution since the origin of basic biological forms. Thus the scientist who accepts the Genesis creation record owes no one an apology.

CHAPTER 6

Hybridization

The term *hybridization* is used to designate both narrow crosses and wide crosses. The progeny of such narrow crosses as that of black guinea pigs with white guinea pigs and of tall garden peas with short garden peas are referred to as hybrids. The same word is used in referring to results of crosses as wide as that between the radish and the cabbage, rye and wheat, lion and tiger, swan and goose.

The English evolutionist Hurst has written that "one of the most remarkable proofs of the influence of crossbreeding in evolution lies in the extensive range of new varieties which have been produced by means of crossings and hybridizations in our domesticated animals and cultivated plants. Of course many changes here result from mutations and transmutations, as in all organisms, but a great deal of the variety is due to new recombinations by crossbreeding and the careful selection of the progeny. Some authors do not consider these results to have any significance in evolution, since most of them have been caused by man's intervention and human selection. On the other hand, however, they give definite proof of the capabilities of organisms to change in all directions; and one must realize that in many cases abnormalities and even monstrosities have been selected as more useful or fanciful for the breeder's purposes, while the more normal mutational changes have been discarded as not being of sufficient interest."[1]

In Hurst's reference to evolution, he uses the word to indicate the production of increased complexity through the origin of varieties within already established kinds and not to the appearance of new kinds. That is, the evolution to which he refers is microevolution, not macroevolution.

Hybridization has resulted in the origin of many interesting groups. Some evident cases of natural origin of new intratypal species were given in the last chapter. The fact that new modern species have been formed by hybridization in the recent past is further established by the following four illustrations in new plant species. These illustrate creationistically defined microevolution, because in each case the cross was within a single basic type, and the hybrid was unquestionably also of the same basic kind as its parents:

1. In 1881 Judge J. H. Logan, of California, introduced the loganberry, *Rubus loganobaccus*, as a cross between the red raspberry, *R. idaeus* or *R. idaeus strigosus*, and the blackberry, *R. allegheniensis*.[2] The loganberry breeds true with no segregation of blackberry and raspberry characters. Some claim this berry was a variety of the dewberry, *R. canadensis;* others, that it is a hybrid between the dewberry and the red raspberry. The weight of opinion, however, is now for the red raspberry-blackberry cross. Regardless of which of these three possibilities is correct, it illustrates the results of hybridization. It is apparent that the loganberry is a true modern species resulting from hybridization and the duplication of chromosomes.[3]

2. Pellew and Newton, in 1929, reported the appearance of a new species of primrose, *Primula kewensis*, at Kew, England, as the result of a spontaneous crossing of *P. verticillata* (eighteen chromosomes) and *P. floribunda* (eighteen chromosomes). The new and fertile species had double the

HYBRIDIZATION 69

number of chromosomes and the combined characters of both the parent species.[4]

3. Goodspeed and Clausen, in 1925, produced a species of tobacco, *Nicotiana digluta* (seventy-two chromosomes), by crossing *N. glutinosa* (twenty-four chromosomes) with *N. tabacum* (forty-eight chromosomes). Since it has the attributes of a true species, it has been given a specific name, *N. digluta*.

4. A pink-flowered horse chestnut, *Aesculus carnea*, was produced by crossing *A. pavia* (forty chromosomes) with *A. hippocastanum* (forty chromosomes). The hybrid, with a complement of eighty chromosomes, is fertile and commonly propagated from seeds.[5]

It is of great importance to observe the fact illustrated here that the most that hybridization can do in the matter of change is to give rise to another variant, in these instances called "new species," within some already existing kind. This is *not* evolution in the sense that evolutionists use it in their theory. Rather, these are merely cases of microevolution as defined by creationists.

The search of past records for cases of hybridization is accompanied by constant danger of deception. Even scientists, whom we sometimes consider to be thick-skinned and thereby immune to popular notions of their day because of their *adherence to facts,* have written untrustworthy accounts of many biological phenomena. The older records of hybridization are commonly unreliable though attested by usually reputable scientists. The superstitions of the day repeatedly find their way into such literature. In his sober paper on "Hybridity in Animals and Plants," read before the Academy of Natural Sciences of Philadelphia in 1846, S. G. Morton records the production of offspring from the natural cross of a bull with a sheep.[6] Every now and then rumors float around regarding a common sheep-pig cross in northwest Mexico, but these were branded as false by the *Live Stock Journal.*[7]

Another prevalent rumor is that cats and rabbits will cross. However no true hybrid between such animals, or between the dog and the cat, has ever been demonstrated. Anyone who endeavored to check all such stories that get into print could be quite busy. According to one account, "Mary L. Morland, Indianapolis," reported that the "fur-fowl," is fairly common in Indiana. This report appeared in a letter published in *Time,* vol. XLVII, no. 15, 1946, in a letter to the magazine. The "fur-fowl" was said to be a cross between a New Zealand red hare and a buff Orpington hen. A letter of inquiry to "Mary" returned unclaimed, but the Indianapolis Chamber of Commerce replied as follows: "In reply to your letter of May 21, we wish to advise that we, also, are unable to locate Mary L. Morland. We contacted a local hatchery and breeding farm and were informed that there is no fowl known as a New Zealand red hare, and that a cross breeding such as mentioned is not known in this locality."

The following month *Time* (May 20, 1946) printed a letter describing a cross in northern Sweden between a hare and a capercaillie (a grouselike bird) with a *picture* of this "skvader." A letter of inquiry received a prompt answer from Hans Bagger, who admitted that it was all a practical joke. The photograph was of a museum specimen of a hare upon whose sides the wings of a capercaillie had been sewed.

On the front page of the *Denver Post,* December 28, 1947, appeared a picture of a young lady holding a small, rough-haired dog, "George," who looked as if he had been wrestling garbage cans all night. The short article accompanying the picture claimed that this creature was a cross between a Persian-Angora cat (the father) and a Pekingese dog. The hybrid had been accomplished by artificial insemination arranged by a Kearney, Nebraska, veterinarian. The name and Utah address of the young lady were furnished, but she did not answer a letter of inquiry addressed to her, nor did she return it. However, a letter to the Kearney Chamber of Commerce elicited the following reply: "Kearney veterinarians state they know nothing about this and agree with you that such a cross is impossible. Our daily newspaper editor states he was contacted by the Associated Press to verify the *Denver Post* story. After his contacts with Kearney veterinarians, he informed the AP that apparently one of their reporters (AP) concocted the story to gain a little publicity."

Stories of alleged crosses between animals seem to catch the public fancy. They are generally enjoyed, and there are plenty of people who like to give the public more of what it enjoys. Although these letters to *Time* were written just in fun, still it should be noted that the statements appear to be chronicling facts. In years to come, statements of scientists notwithstanding, the average person will *know* that wide crosses occur because he "once saw a *photograph* of a cross between a hare and a bird." Every rumor I have been able to investigate of a supposed cross between organisms so different that they could be considered separate Genesis kinds has turned out as did the "fur-fowl," the "skvader," and "George."

Some people actually believe that the grapefruit originated as a cross between grape and lemon. Probably of the same nature was the report that a new vegetable called a "wobbie" had been developed in Holland from a carrot-beet cross.[8] I once bought a copy of *Bird Hybrids*, 390 pages,[9] thinking I was securing a wealth of information on hybridization among birds, when my eye fell on this note: "As negative results and presumed hybrids, as well as authentic hybrids, have been included, *the listing of a particular cross does not necessarily mean that it has occurred*." Then, when I read the listing of a cross between a domestic hen and a duck, I knew what the author meant. Such a hybrid has never been produced.

Complicating the picture is the possibility that an apparent cross is not a hybrid, but merely a haploid development resulting from chemical stimulation by the sperm. Loeb stated in 1912: "It is therefore possible to cross practically any marine teleost (bony fish) with any other."[10] But it is now known that the phenomenon is merely a parthenogenetic development of the eggs through the activating influence of the foreign sperm. Similar cases have been observed in "crosses" of echinoderms with mollusks, and echinoderms with annelids. Cytological examination has shown that the entire sperm nucleus, in such instances, is thrown out of the egg at the first segmentation division. Centrifuging, treating with certain chemicals, or even merely pricking with a needle has accomplished the same sort of development.

I am of the opinion that the *union* of two gamete nuclei, regardless of the dissimilarity of the individuals from which they come, and regardless of the fact that development may cease in early embryonic stages, is evidence that the parents are members of the same Genesis kind. This assumption is substantiated by all valid breeding data, that true fertilization of the egg occurs only in individuals morphologically similar and thus basically the same kind of organism. If this is true, it would seem that each Genesis kind is made up of a cluster of individuals (races, species, genera, or even families in some cases) originally endowed with the same chemical characteristics. Foreign sperms cannot accomplish fertilization because of chemical incompatibility with the egg. However, mutations and chromosome changes since Creation would accomplish considerable reproductive isolation of groups within each original kind. Thus today we may even find sterility between races of the same species.

HYBRIDIZATION

Regarding hybridization, we read the following from the *Yearbook of Agriculture,* page 183: "There is no way to tell in advance whether two distantly related organisms actually will cross. The attempt must be made, and sometimes it must be repeated many times. Most scientists are guided by the existing classification systems for plants and animals, and formerly there were many crosses they did not attempt because the organisms were too far apart in the classification system. They thought this made the cross impossible. This article mentions several hybrids that were produced only because someone was bold enough to make the attempt and to make it with sufficient numbers to get results. It is to be hoped that more and wider crosses will be tried in the future."[11]

As suggested in this quotation, the physiological species may extend over different taxonomic groups in unexpected ways. In some cases little relation between genetic kinds and systematic groups may exist. In the mind of many creationists a study of the former is the only way to gain an idea of what sorts of units are referred to in Genesis as organisms (plants) made to reproduce after their kinds. However, the modern taxonomic series is merely a useful tool the scientist uses to make himself intelligible to his colleagues when discussing organic forms.

One of the outstanding physiological characteristics of man is his inability to cross with any other kind of animal— even with the chimpanzee. "There is no evidence of the origin of a hybrid between man and any other mammal."[12] For a somewhat extended discussion of why man has never been able to cross with any beast, see my article on hybridization in the *Creation Research Society Quarterly* for June 1973.[13]

Many creationists think this proves that the other Genesis kinds were likewise physiologically isolated. The vast amount of hybridization and attempted hybridization reveals that apparently only in cases where the parents are manifestly similar plants or animals is crossing possible. This indicates to certain creationists that hybridization may be a key to the present-day distribution of the created kinds. They know that *lack* of ability to cross proves nothing conclusively in the matter of kinds, because, as noted above, even races of the same species may be sterile *inter se*. But they do hold that any cases of hybridization, even though they terminate in death in early embryonic stages, are indicative that the parents must be members of the same Genesis kinds. The assumption is that in the original state all the members of the same kinds, possibly corresponding to races, were cross-fertile. Some creationists hold that while all the evolutionists' research performed in an endeavor to discover whether evolution is occurring, is, in view of the statements of Genesis 1 and 2, love's labor lost. Yet hybridizing experiments are valuable, because only in that way can those physiological units called Genesis kinds be even somewhat delimited.

As we have seen, it is possible that two groups of individuals may develop from the same stock and yet prove sterile when mated. Is there, then, any basis in fact for such a conclusion?

When we say these forms "prove to be sterile when mated," we do not refer to the failure to produce offspring which develops from such isolating mechanisms as (a) the failure of individuals to meet because of ecological isolation, ie, they are confined to *different habitats*; (b) the failure to meet due to breeding periods coming at *different times* of the year; or (c) psychological factors, such as differences in scents, courtship behavior, and sexual recognition signs. It is possible that mutational changes could cause any of these reasons for failure to cross. In this way varieties might

HYBRIDIZATION

arise within original kinds. This apparently is the origin of many of the modern species of our day.

This type of physiological change is the specific one which could split one strain off the mother strain by causing chemical incompatibility with the ancestral group. Of course such a change would arise in a single individual, and several generations of inbreeding may follow before a pure strain of the changed form could appear. A number of cases are on record where just such changes have apparently occurred, such as strains of barley, hawk's beard (*Crepis*), and *Drosophila*. In chapter three we have already referred to the case of race A and race B in *Drosophila pseudoobscura*, and the two morphologically identical, though intersterile, species, *D. equinoxialis* and *D. willistoni*.

Chromosome changes serve to cause cross-sterility among the members of the Genesis kind. Translocation, for example, is known to cause abortion of a part of the pollen and ovules. In some plants, as Dobzhansky points out, the resulting semisterility is used as a method for the detection of translocations.[14] Dobzhansky also speaks of the new strain of *Drosophila melanogaster* produced by Kozhevnikov by combining two strains characterized by different translocations.[15] Kozhevnikov appropriately called this new strain *D. artificialis*. He found that it bred true within its own kind but was sterile when crossed with *D. melanogaster*, from which it was developed. In the preceding chapter, reference was made to the possible function of polyploidy in the development of sterility between races of a single kind. Goldschmidt says of this: "But there is a phenomenon which occasionally produces isolation through chromosomal differences; namely polyploidy."[16]

Thus research in this field reveals a mechanism in nature whereby different groups of the same kind of organism may become cross-sterile. These data indicate that many of the species within present-day kinds, even though they may be cross-sterile, have possibly developed within the original kinds since Creation. The scientific mind welcomes facts, but it is extremely important to recognize here that even though physiological discontinuity between groups may have developed, still this fact does not open the door for the evolution of new kinds from existing kinds. The modern species which may have developed in this way are still as clearly bona fide members of their kind as were the members of the group from which they sprang. To illustrate, the dog and the fox are almost universally sterile when crossed, yet this fact does not necessarily mean that they represent two separately created kinds, nor does it indicate that evolution of new kinds is occurring. Dogs and foxes are obviously members of a single major kind. Whether one holds that they are originally created races of the original dog kind, or whether he believes that they have developed since Creation from other members of the dog kind, is a matter of personal preference.

It has been the attitude of evolutionists and of some creationists that the discovery of isolating mechanisms in nature would be proof positive that evolution had occurred. The English evolutionist Bateson declared that the proof of the development of this cross-sterility is the event "for which we wait." Historically, some creationists have felt that such a mechanism must not be recognized in nature. However, if certain processes exist in nature, they should be recognized regardless of personal theories. Real proof *does* exist in support of the idea that cross-sterility *may* develop between closely related forms.

The danger here is not in the recognition of development of cross-sterility, but rather in the personal interpretation of what this process can accomplish in the matter of variation. It is clear that in all known cases where such sterility has

HYBRIDIZATION

developed, the races or variants which have been formed are *just as completely members of the single kind to which their ancestors belonged as were their ancestors*. The peculiar pattern of each kind is so extremely complex and persistent as to resist serious disfigurement even when at the mercy of the combined effects of *all* the processes of change.

The evolutionist is unduly optimistic over the degree of change that can occur in the most mutable of kinds. He feels that even though it can be seriously doubted that even a good species can originate from these processes today, still just give these forces of change sufficient time, say a few million years, and changes *will* occur which will erect new kinds from other kinds. He tells us that we in our short span of time are merely viewing a very few frames of a moving picture. Although the changes we view are usually small, yet given more time those changes will create new kinds.

The evolutionist fails on the same point on which Darwin failed—failure to recognize that we live in a law-bound universe. He does not recognize that natural forces and principles have their limitations and do not change through the years. Gravity can do certain things, but it has bounds. We cannot lift ourselves by our own bootstraps today; if we would keep at it for a few million years, we still could not accomplish it. The law of action and reaction does not change as the ages roll. Apparently neither do processes of variation in organisms. No one can explain all the differences between two original kinds of plants or animals; yet that these differences are real and of such a nature as never to be eliminated through processes of change is witnessed by every work of research conducted to test the nature of these phenomena.

Authentic records show that crossing has taken place at least to the extent of beginning of embryonic development

78 VARIATION AND FIXITY IN NATURE

between the following more common animals: lion and tiger (liger, tiglon); stallion and jenny ass (hinny); jackass and mare (mule); horse and zebra (zebroid); kiang and onager (kianager); dogs, wolves, jackals, coyotes, and some foxes; mouse and rat; sheep and goat; chicken and guinea fowl; *Bos* bull and zebu or Brahman (Santa Gertrudis); *Bos* bull and American bison or "buffalo," and European bison or Auroch (catalo); *Bos* bull, gaur, yak, gayal, banteng, and kouprey; swan and goose (swoose); and house martin and barn swallow.

Hybrids among animals are frequent across gaps which may not appear so wide. Illustrations of this type of crossing are offered in the hybrids among species of ducks, pigeons, and pheasants. Also between purple and bronzed grackles; red-shafted and yellow-shafted flicker; different species of the Cecropia moth; crow; western and eastern species of European hedgehog; species of toads; house (English) sparrow and the willow sparrow; some species of warblers; several species of freshwater fish; some species of gall wasps; rabbits and hares; species of ibex; species of caribou; and so on.

Among plants some of the widest crosses for which we have authentic records are those of wheat with wheat grass, goat grass, boat grass, and rye; corn with teosinte and gamagrass; radish with cabbage; sugarcane with sorghum; fescue grass with Italian rye grass; wild tobacco with petunia; bean with cow pea; blackberry with raspberry.

It is known that species within the following plant genera will cross with other species of the same genus and produce hybrids: alder, arbutus, basswood, birch, buckeye, canna, carnation, catalpa, catchfly, chestnut, cotton, currant and gooseberry, darnel, dogwood, elm, evening primrose, fir, four-o'clock, goat grass, hawk's beard, hawthorne, hemlock, hickory, holly, honey locust, larch, lily, black locust,

HYBRIDIZATION

magnolia, maple, oak, oats, onion, papaw, pea, pine, poplar, poppy, rose, snapdragon, spiderwort, spruce, sycamore, timothy grass, tobacco, vetch, wheat, willow, and yew.

It will be observed that the individuals concerned in each cross belong to the same large group, a group with members bound together by fundamental similarities in morphology. For the theory which holds that Genesis kinds were smaller groups and that crossing of kinds was possible, it is unfortunate that in all authentic cases of hybridization the hybridizing individuals are obviously members of the same large group, such as the man kind, the cow kind, the dog kind, or the bean kind. Thus, after many centuries, crossing still appears to occur only within the borders of the well-defined kind.

Usually a striking correlation exists between breeding performance and nearness in our systematic catalogs. Even the radish and the cabbage stand close together in our classification system. In other words, compatible physiological characters seem to be accompanied with similar morphological characters, but the converse is not always true. That is why our present-day systematic lists cannot always be taken as correct pictures of actual blood relationships of organisms.

Thus hybridization deserves an important place among those factors which produce variants among plants and animals. However, its limitations must be observed. The fact that crossing cannot occur across basic types but is in each instance confined to the members of a single kind, makes it of no further service than to increase the complexity within separate kinds. Experimental facts show that isolating mechanisms in nature never accomplish more than to increase the diversity within the original kind.

CHAPTER 7

What Does the Fossil Record Tell Us?

Most evolutionists agree that there is one place to go to see what they think demonstrates evolution as a biological fact. That place is in the fossil-bearing rocks. At present geologists are of the opinion that the sedimentary layers, those which contain the fossils, may extend downward as much as twelve miles, although man has actually never penetrated these layers more deeply than some 25,000 feet—nearly five miles. This depth was reached in an oil well in the Mississippi River delta. An oil well in Oklahoma reportedly reached a depth of 27,000 feet.

Because of the phenomenon of discontinuity among living plants and animals, with no connecting links between basic types, no real proof of evolution in the present prevails. In other words, it is impossible in the living world to prove in an empirical way that organic evolution has occurred. This opinion was made quite clear to me in a letter from Dobzhansky under date of December 22, 1944. He wrote: "When one says that evolution is established beyond reasonable doubt, one obviously does not mean that one can see evolution happen and reproduce it in a test tube, but this is the evidence which you escape by your device of saying that it is all change merely within a 'kind.' What you are after is evidently evidence for the thing which is called by this rather unfortunate term 'macroevolution.' Now, this is a

WHAT DOES THE FOSSIL RECORD TELL US? 81

process taking place in geological time, hence it, as any other historical process (human or natural), can be proven or disproven only by inference from the available evidence."

In order to help the student of origins decide which of the two hypotheses of origins, special creation or organic evolution, may be the most in keeping with the facts, we will briefly survey the situation among the fossils. The student should study this material carefully, for evolutionists say that here among the fossils resides the only real evidence for macroevolution. But note the following admissions:

Arnold says: "It has long been hoped that extinct plants will ultimately reveal some of the stages through which existing groups have passed during the course of their development, but it must be freely admitted that this aspiration has been fulfilled to a very slight extent, even though paleobotanical research has been in progress for more than one hundred years. As yet we have not been able to trace the phylogenetic history of a single group of modern plants from its beginning to the present."[1]

Darrah: "No fossil representative thus far recognized suggests that ancient bryophytes were very different from living forms."[2]

Andrews: "The spore-bearing organs of these Permian mosses have not been found, so that more precise comparisons with living forms are not possible. Their importance lies in the fact that they are well-preserved, they are unquestionably mosses, and sufficiently similar to modern ones in their vegetative organization as to suggest no major changes in moss evolution since that time."[3]

Tutin: "In the ninety-two years [written in 1952] since the publication of the *Origin of Species* a great deal of argument but remarkably little fact has been produced about the relationships of the Angiosperms (flowering plants).... Meanwhile, neither paleobotany, morphology, anatomy, or cytology has thrown any light on the origin of the Angiosperms or of any major group within the Angiosperms which an unbiased observer can regard as unequivocal. Indeed, one may go further and say that no more is known about the origin of any major groups of plants than was known in 1859."[4]

Clark: "When we examine a series of fossils of any age, we may pick out one and say with confidence, 'This is a crustacean'—or starfish, or a brachiopod, or annelid, or any other type of creature as the case may be. . . .

"Since all the fossils are determinable as members of their respective groups by application of definitions of those groups drawn up from and based entirely on living types, and since none of these definitions of the phyla or major groups of animals need be in any way altered or expanded to include the fossils, it naturally follows that throughout the fossil record these major groups have remained essentially unchanged. This means that the interrelationships between them likewise have remained unchanged."[5]

Beerbower: "All [crinoid echinoderms] are distinct at their first appearance." "On the other hand, they [vertebrates] are pretty well diversified at their first appearance." "Unfortunately most of the connection forms [fishes] are still listed among the 'missing links.' " "These two, the sharks and the bony fishes, were distinct at their first appearance in the fossil record."[6]

Romer: "The chances of obtaining a complete graded series (if one existed) are hence obviously vastly less than in the case of more normal phyletic evolution. 'Links' are missing just where we most fervently desire them, and it is all too probable that many 'links' will continue to be missing."[7]

Newell: "These finds [of assumed connecting links] are, however, rare; and experience shows that the gaps which separate the highest categories may never be bridged in the

WHAT DOES THE FOSSIL RECORD TELL US?

fossil record. Many of the discontinuities tend to be more and more emphasized with increased collection."[8]

Davis: "The sudden emergence of major adaptive types, as seen in the abrupt appearance in the fossil record of families and orders, continued to give trouble. The phenomenon lay in the genetical no man's land beyond the limits of experimentation. A few paleontologists even today cling to the idea that these gaps will be closed by further collecting, i.e., that they are accidents of sampling; but most regard the observed discontinuities as real and have sought an explanation for them.

"But the facts of paleontology conform equally well with other interpretations that have been discredited by neobiological works, e.g., divine creation, innate developmental processes, Lamarckism, etc., and paleontology by itself can neither prove nor refute such ideas."[9]

Simpson: "As it became more and more evident that the great gaps remained, despite wonderful progress in finding the members of lesser transitional groups and progressive lines, it was no longer satisfactory to impute this absence of objective data entirely to chance. The failure of paleontology to produce such evidence was so keenly felt that a few disillusioned naturalists even decided that the theory of organic evolution, or of general organic continuity of descent, was wrong, after all."[10]

"In spite of these examples, it remains true, as every paleontologist knows, that most new species, genera, and families, and that nearly all new categories above the level of families, appear in the record suddenly and are not led up to by known, gradual, completely continuous transitional sequences."[11]

"The facts are that many species and genera, indeed the majority, do appear suddenly in the fossil record, differing sharply and in many ways from earlier groups, and that this appearance of discontinuity becomes more common the higher the level, until it is virtually universal as regards orders and all higher steps. . . .

"The face of the record thus does really suggest normal discontinuity at all levels, most particularly at high levels, and some paleontologists . . . insist on taking the record at this face value. Others . . . discount this evidence completely and maintain that the breaks neither prove nor suggest that there is any normal mode of evolution other than that seen in continuously evolving and abundantly recorded groups. This essentially paleontological problem is also of crucial interest for all other biologists, and since there is such a conflict of opinion, nonpaleontologists may choose either to believe the authority who agrees with their prejudices or to discard the evidence as worthless."[12]

The above quotations are but a sample of what the student finds all through paleontological literature. This state of the fossil evidence will come as a shock to those who have thought that fossils constituted the strongest evidence for organic evolution. After all, the discontinuity between basic types which makes it impossible to demonstrate evolution among living things also exists among the fossils. Only when this situation is viewed through powerful faith-in-evolution lenses is any argument at all for evolution attempted from the fossil record.

The creationist, however, finds the same harmony between the discontinuous kinds of fossils and the Genesis account of origins that he found among living plants and animals. The few assumed connecting links, such as *Archaeopteryx,* were no doubt reasonably discrete created kinds; and the series of fossil horses and elephants and camels were ecological races that lived upon earth at the time of the great Deluge.

We cannot devote space here to the matter of the radioac-

WHAT DOES THE FOSSIL RECORD TELL US?

tive time clock, which, in the case of the Cambrian period, is believed to date fossil-bearing strata at some 600 million years. Indeed these radioactive data do seem to show a diminishing age from Cambrian at the bottom to Recent at the top. But the creationist point of view holds that a universal flood prevailed a millennium and one-half after Creation week, and the sediments laid down in that unnatural deluge would naturally be oldest at the bottom and youngest at the top. That this very situation involving movement of water and earth, combined with extensive volcanism, would have effects upon radioactive materials which would largely disrupt any time-recording function, has been revealed in the recent research of Dalrymple and Moore,[13] and Noble and Naughton[14] with single lava flows in the Hawaiian Islands. Differences in ages of as much as twenty-two million years in the same flow were found because of variations in hydrostatic pressure and rate of cooling. Such findings, together with the undemonstrable assumptions upon which all radioactive datings are based, should make every careful student guarded in his acceptance of ages so based.

Creationists and evolutionists, then, differ on just what the fossil-bearing strata actually represent. According to the evolutionist view, the undisturbed fossil layers portray a fairly complete history of the span of organic evolution; while to the creationist the major portion of the fossils are remains of organisms which were mostly living at one time, the time of Noah's Flood, with the addition of such fossils as chanced to form during the forty-odd centuries since the great Flood.

This to the creationist means that trilobites and brachiopods of the Cambrian were living at the same time as the dinosaurs of the Triassic and Jurassic. To the creationist the greater part of the geologic column is telescoped into the antediluvian period. When the student studies the account of the Noachian Deluge recorded in Genesis 6 to 8 and begins to comprehend the nature of this universal cataclysm in which water, wind, earth movements, and volcanism were employed *unnaturally* to accomplish the destruction of the earth's surface to a great depth, he perceives how unprofitable it may be to invoke uniformitarian principles in an effort to explain this or that specific phenomenon in the surface of the earth. Real evidence for the truth of the telescoping of the geologic column is furnished in the facts presented in the portrayal made by paleontologist Clark earlier in this chapter.

CHAPTER 8

Fixity Among Living Things

As we study the Old Testament in an effort to discover what it teaches on the matter of origins, we find that on Days Three, Five, and Six, plants and animals were created from the substances of the earth, after their kinds. On Day Three all kinds of plants appeared, varying in form and structure from giants of the forest to the lichens adorning their bark to violets blooming at their feet. They varied from minute ocean plankton and lowly carpeting land types and herbaceous forms to fruit-bearing trees. At the close of Day Six all kinds of animals swam in the water, burrowed in the soil, crept, walked, and skipped lightly upon the land, climbed the trees, and flew through the air. The Genesis text apparently indicates that every basic type of organism was in existence by the close of the sixth day.

A study of the lists of clean and unclean animals in Leviticus 11 reveals that the Hebrew word *min*, kind, in some cases may be so restricted in scope as even to suggest the possibility of creation of smaller groups inside larger groups, as for instance the distinguishing of the falcon kind (v. 14) from the hawk kind (v. 16) within the larger group of diurnal birds of prey and in delimiting the bald locust kind from the locust kind (v. 22). Thus when Genesis says that kinds were created, it may not necessarily mean that only the very large basic types were represented on the earth at the close of Creation, but the word translated "kind" may also refer to the creation of at least some of the constituent subordinate groups. At any rate, Genesis 2:1 tells us that by the close of the sixth day God had finished, completed His work of creating. Because of the physiological constitution of the created groups, the quota of basic types of living things was filled before the setting of the sun on the evening of the sixth day; so from that time onward, except by the interposition of the Creator Himself, no new basic kinds could appear upon the earth.

When the scientist or anyone else reads Genesis, he should use care lest he add words not actually spelled out there. This adding of words was done by many theologians during the century preceding the publication of Darwin's *Origin of Species*. These scholastics represented Genesis as stating that both plants and animals brought forth (reproduced) after their kinds. Occasionally modern scientists read Genesis in the same way.

A careful reading of Genesis 1 and 2 reveals that no assertion in just so many words is made regarding the reproductive behavior of the created kinds of animals. However, with regard to the plants we read in Genesis 1:11, 12, RSV: "The earth brought forth vegetation, plants yielding seed according to their own kinds." The student may wish to review the discussion of this point in chapter three.

Some feel that because Genesis *does not* state in so many words that animals brought forth after their own kinds, and because they think nothing is said about how plants reproduced, therefore Genesis gives no clues on their reproductive behavior. However, God did not leave the problem as indefinite as that. A point in Genesis too often overlooked is the statement, repeated at least ten times in the first chapter, to the effect that plants and animals were created *after their kinds*. This repeated assertion gives us an important key to what was created and to the reproductive characteristics of these groups of organisms. If the record had merely said, "God created plants and animals," the topic would have been left open so that man could surmise almost anything he wished, so long as he remembered that God made their ancestors. But as we have noted above, we are told quite in detail that *all kinds* of plants appeared on Day Three, and that *all kinds* of animals appeared on Days Five and Six. Possibly only he who has studied the laws of reproduction of kinds of organisms can comprehend the specific and satisfactory nature of the Genesis account when it records that *kinds* were created before the close of Day Six and that God then *ended* His work, which had included the creation of all the kinds.

How do we identify the different kinds of plants and animals? How do we tell a pumpkin from an oak, a mole from an elephant? Not one of us is so self-depreciating as to feel that he could not distinguish these kinds. But how *do* we distinguish them? By observing their differences in size, in form, in structure, and in growth habit. These distinguishing characters become manifest in each kind as it develops from the fertilized egg. The pumpkin becomes a pumpkin and an oak an oak because of the chemical differences in the hereditary determiners, the genes, the DNA in the nuclei of the cells. The pumpkin is limited in its reproduction to the production of individuals of the pumpkin kind only because of the specific and peculiar chemical quality of its hereditary substances. This is true of all the kinds, pumpkins, oaks, moles, elephants, and all. Every man who has studied reproduction at all, and even those who have been normally observant, know that if kinds are present then there is a reproductive behavior in each kind which makes it capable of producing only individuals of the same basic kind, a reproductive behavior which sets it apart in both present and future from all other kinds. Thus the man kind has from Creation produced and will continue to produce to the end of time only human beings, which cannot be crossed or confused with any other kind. Thus we recognize that Genesis *does teach a fixity* which has continued since Creation week. But the fixity is not at the level of the *individual* so as to make offspring as like their parents as coins stamped out by the same dies, but rather at the level of the *kind* so that new individuals are never anything other than of the same kind as their parents. For example, the fixity is at the level of the dog kind and not at the level of the kinds of dogs. The variation that can occur within some kinds is amazing, and we are delighted as we study the many varieties of men, dogs, cats, pigeons, finches, tortoises, roses, gladiolus, irises, bluegrass, and hawthorn trees. But the farther we push our investigation the clearer the natural principle becomes that kinds can reproduce only after their kinds. This biological research illuminates the statements of Genesis and demonstrates that at Creation the Creator did create a fixity into the world of living things by creating *all kinds* of plants and animals.

Nothing in the Creation account denies the possibility that in some instances subordinate groups may have been created in the kinds. We speculate rather harmlessly that the horse, the ass, and the zebra could illustrate one such case, and that within the rose kind (not the *Rosaceae* or rose family of the botanist with its pears, apples, juneberries, hawthorns, strawberries, raspberries, blackberries, dewberries, cinquefoils, agrimony, plums, cherries, etc., but the cultivated rose of the rose breeder) the Creator may have beautified the earth with many cross-fertile strains of roses. Because the respective kinds of plants and animals continue through all generations due to the peculiar, specific, and isolating chemical qualities within each kind, it would

FIXITY AMONG LIVING THINGS

be expected to find that the varying members of a kind would all have very nearly the same chemical constitution. This would make them incompatible when crossed with individuals of other kinds but usually compatible and crossable with other varieties of the same kind. In many instances, even after these many generations of mutational change and deterioration, the Genesis kind and the modern biological species would be identical.

According to the Genesis account, a *fixity* was built into the world of living things by a creation of organisms *in all their kinds*. It would indeed appear to be a strange divine activity which would produce hundreds of thousands of kinds of plants and animals and make no provision to prevent an immediate welter of hybridization which would soon obliterate the lovely, diversified pattern of creation. Genesis leaves the student of origins facing no dilemma in the matter of how much evolution has occurred among plants and animals. He learns that no genetic relationship exists between the diverse basic types of our day. Their similarity in design is the handiwork of an omniscient, omnipotent Creator with a master plan.

CHAPTER 9

The Form and Structure of Living Things *

The scientist who accepts the origin of plants and animals depicted in Genesis 1 and 2 has a vastly different concept of comparative anatomy from one who believes that all living things have developed from single-celled organisms. Most evolutionists hold the concept that *all* organisms are genetically related; therefore the more closely living things resemble each other in body line or chemistry, the closer is their genetic relationship.

Contrastingly, most creationists believe that there is no genetic relationship between basic types; any resemblance among these created kinds was the result of a materialized plan once existent in the mind of the Creator. To the impartial mind (if there be such a wonder in the natural world and if it remains purely theoretical) these doctrines would be equally logical and reasonable.

What is the *origin* of the form and structure with which comparative anatomy is concerned? According to Hebrew Scriptures, plants and then animals appeared instantaneously in all their intriguing forms as the result of the Creator's fiat.

In Genesis 1:11, 12, the created forms of plants are desig-

---

*The author has adapted this material from his article which, under the same title, appeared in *Creation Research Society Annual*, vol. 6, no. 1, June 1969, pp. 13-25.

THE FORM AND STRUCTURE OF LIVING THINGS

nated as grass (*deshe*, whose root signifies "to be damp"), herbs (*eseb*, herbage), and trees (*ets peri*, tree of fruit). These three broad groups evidently include all vegetation. The first group possibly does not include grass as we know it, but may refer to mosses, liverworts, lichens, and other carpeting plants.

The translation of the Greek Septuagint notwithstanding, members of the second group are obviously distinct from those of the first, as borne out by 2 Kings 19:26 and Isaiah 37:27, where they are again mentioned separately. Also members of this group are prominent as seed bearers.

It is this group, *eseb*, which Genesis 1:29 says have been given to man along with fleshy fruits and nuts as his food. The KJV translation of Genesis 3:18, "herb of the field" (RSV: "plants of the field"; NEB: "none but wild plants for you to eat"), possibly describes an additional type of food given to man after his sin, and is from this same *eseb*. *Eseb* is also used in Deuteronomy 11:15 to describe the food of cattle. Thus this second group appears to include all plants between mosses, liverworts, lichens, ferns, and other nonseed-bearing plants, and the woody shrubs and trees.

Ets peri, tree of fruit, the term covering the third group, is a singular collective that stands for woody plants bearing dry nuts and cones or fleshy fruits such as berries, drupes, and pomes.

These three broad groups do not coincide with modern classifications of plants, but for the nonscientist they paint the picture of the origin of vegetation—the lowly forms, the taller herbaceous forms, and the woody shrubs and trees.

Genesis 1:11, 12 says that in the span of a single day consisting of one period of darkness and one of light—a solar, 24-hour day—the Creator brought the basic kinds of plants into existence. This vegetation includes seed-bearing plants which evolutionists affirm to be the most highly and recently evolved forms. This special revelation was given to man so that he might know that every distinct kind of plant that ever lived on the earth was formed on Day Three of Creation week.

Here, with regard to the plants, not only does Genesis describe the origin of basic types or kinds, but it also makes clear the appearance of the succeeding generations of each kind. "The earth brought forth vegetation, plants yielding seed according to their own kinds." Genesis 1:12, RSV. Because of their fiat origin and reproductive behavior there was no way that evolution of new basic types could occur.

Some students of origins, those who could be called theists, will agree to this last sentence with regard to *natural* processes. But they hold that now and then down through millions of years the Creator caused organisms to bring forth unnaturally so as to produce new basic types and in this way derive the more complex from the simpler. That God *could* have done this the Bible-believing Christian will agree. But in the same breath he will point out that the Holy Scriptures know no such derivative type of origins.

The statement that the Creator commanded the earth to bring forth the plants "according to their own kinds," and that the earth *did* bring forth the plants "according to their own kinds," apparently means in part that He formed plants after some orderly plan. This plan apparently was not discovered by such plant taxonomists as Adolf Engler, Charles Bessey, or John Hutchinson. These taxonomists based their systems of plant classification on efforts to answer such evolutionist questions as the following: "How are these plants related? From what are they descended? Which characters are those of ancestrally more primitive plants and which ones are derived from them? Which characters have longest remained unchanged? Have characters arisen only once, or have some arisen many times independent of one another?" These questions are listed by C. H. M. Lawrence, a Cornell taxonomist.[1]

These early botanists brushed aside the inspired account of distinctly separate beginnings of plant kinds and concluded instead that all basic types of plants are genetically related. The term "phylogeny," race history or development of a kind of organism, appeared in the literature as attempts were made to place together those families thought to be more closely related genetically, with assumed derivative groups following those taken for granted to be ancestral.

However none of these efforts has produced a truly phylogenetic system. Not one discovery of plant paleontology has revealed this elusive evidence that evolutionists seek—evidence that truly primitive forms once existed. Therefore the taxonomist is frustrated in not knowing which characters are primitive and which are advanced. An acceptance of Genesis would have saved a vast amount of work through its revelation of the natural truth that there is neither "primitive" nor "advanced"—rather that all basic kinds appeared simultaneously upon the earth.

In botany this attempt to follow the *ignis fatuus* of evolution has resulted in the three systems mentioned above, plus the system of Pulle of Utrecht, that of Skottsberg of Stockholm, and at least a score of other classification systems which confuse those who classify plants. The situation would suggest a return to a point of view similar to that of Linnaeus, the father of taxonomy, a creationist. Even with *complete* avoidance of the concept of genetic relationship existing among basic kinds, almost endless interesting groupings and subgroupings of plants can be made based purely upon comparative anatomy.

Although we may have departed somewhat from the subject of form and structure into taxonomy, we are still discussing comparative anatomy. Plant classification systems are based entirely upon the form and structure of the plants. Therefore, our philosophy of comparative anatomy will influence our procedure in the science of classification. The Bible-believing student of comparative anatomy of animals turns first to Genesis for the orientation necessary. The translation of the Hebrew found in KJV and RSV, Genesis 1:20, is unclear in that it appears to state that both water animals and (in KJV) flying forms were brought forth *by the waters*; but in Genesis 2:19 we read that "every fowl of the air" was formed "out of the ground." The translation in Genesis 1:20 in the NEB is consistently correct here, "Let the waters teem with countless living creatures." With regard to the fowls, both the RSV ("let birds fly above the earth across the firmament of the heavens"), and NEB ("let birds fly above the earth across the vault of heaven") agree in their translation. Interestingly the Greek Septuagint translates this portion, "every creature that flies with wings," thus broadening the meaning until it could include bats and pterodactyls.

In other words, in Genesis 1 no statement is made regarding the material used in the formation of water animals and flying forms. However, it is made clear that on Day Five all water animals and flying forms were brought forth in all their kinds and were shaped into discrete kinds and present abundantly at the close of Day Five.

Every water animal and flying form, whether starfish or mollusk, sponge or porpoise, jellyfish or whale, hummingbird or teratornis, butterfly or pterodactyl—all kinds were patterned according to their distinct morphological differences. No room is left for supposition that these discrete kinds derived from other kinds of more simple morphology.

The use of the expression *wayyibera*, "and he created," Genesis 1:21, seems puzzling at first reading. Why should

THE FORM AND STRUCTURE OF LIVING THINGS

God *make* plants and *create* water animals and flying forms? The word for create may be used here for at least two reasons. First, verse 21 says that God caused animals to swarm in the waters without saying they were formed from any material. Therefore, a form of *bara*, to create, was used. Second, *bara* is used where the idea of novelty is to be conveyed (see Isaiah 41:20; 48:6, 7; 65:17; Jeremiah 31:22). To bring into existence such remarkable creatures which breathe and are animated and can go where they wish is worthy of the term *bara*.

Genesis 1:24, 25 records the origin on Day Six of the dry-land animals. In the origin of these creatures, as in the case of the plants on Day Three, we have a mediate creation. Instead of directly calling land creatures forth by His word, the Creator temporarily enables the earth to produce them. The "why" we may not perceive, but we do know that they came from the dust and upon death return to dust. The command to the earth is "cause to come forth" (from the Hebrew verb *tose*). This command is identical with the statement in verse 12 regarding the earth "causing" the plants "to go out."

The Scripture says the land animals appeared in three groups, each group name being in the singular collective. First are the *behemah* or "domestic animals," often called cattle. The root for *behemah* means "to be dumb"—dumb brute. This characteristic does not set any group apart, however, because all animals lack the power of articulate speech.

The second group are the *remes*, from a root "to move about lightly" or "glide about." The translations in both the KJV and the RSV, "creeping things" (NEB says "reptiles") is too narrow because it does not leave room for the larger land reptiles and amphibians. It would appear that *remes* includes everything that moves on the ground as snakes, or close to the ground as spiders and lizards.

The third group is *chayyath ha' ares*. The original comes from the root *chay*, "living," suggesting vital energy and activity, then the modifying phrase "of the earth" is added. Members of this group are in a sense different from the other two groups because they have freedom of movement and may be designated as "wild beasts of the earth."

This classification of land animals was never intended to satisfy a taxonomically inclined biologist, but it is satisfactory in that it gives a picture sufficient to call to mind all types of land animals. A point given the highest emphasis in the account is that the Creator, obviously with a plan in mind which included all kinds of land animals, commanded the earth to produce these basic kinds. This part of the account closes (verse 25) with the assertion that all these kinds planned in the mind of God took form instantaneously by His power, without genetic relationship, on Day Six. "And God saw that it was good."

In a discussion of physical form and structure man should be included. The account of man's origin occupies two verses in Genesis 1, verses 26 and 27. The singular dignity of man and his position as the crowning work of creation is evidenced in two ways: (1) by the divine council held before his formation; (2) by the fact that he alone of the entire creation was patterned after his Maker. (We hear objections that some Christian is picturing God under a human form—"too anthropomorphic!" We inquire, If man was created "in the image of God," should God not, at least in a general way, resemble a man?)

The narration rises to a solemn chant in the words (RSV), "So God created man in his own image, in the image of God he created him; male and female he created them." The Lord Jesus Christ accepted this account of man's origin as simple history. In Matthew 19:4-6 (also Mark 10:6-8) He

THE FORM AND STRUCTURE OF LIVING THINGS

makes direct reference to the literal Genesis account of the origin of man.

The threefold use of *bara*, "create," in Genesis 1:27, is significant here. *Bara* is appropriate because, as in verse 1, something is brought into being which did not formerly exist; second, as in verse 21, something is being endowed with life; also, because a creature with the endowments of man formed in God's image is entirely new.

Man's physical body is, of course, similar to that of the mammals. Genesis tells us that man was made of the same substance as the animals: the dust of the ground. Furthermore, his food (Genesis 1:29) was identical to that of the beasts of the field. He moved in the same physical environment, and the mechanics of his activities were much like those of the higher animals. Thus man's comparative anatomy today does not coerce him into acceptance of a bestial origin, but rather harmonizes with the biblical account of special creation.

It is clear in Genesis that God commanded the earth to bring forth plants (Genesis 1:11) and animals (Genesis 1:24). Just how long this command was to remain in force was apparently unclear in the minds of theologians of the Middle Ages. Probably confusion resulted from the effort to accept both Aristotle and Genesis at the same time. These theologians taught in the universities that spontaneous generation was a natural fact. The scholastics reasoned that God had commanded the earth to bring forth living organisms, so in the Middle Ages the earth was understood to be obeying that command faithfully.

We marvel that these Bible students pondered origins as presented in Genesis and yet seem to have missed that part of the account found in the first two verses of Genesis 2. Here we read, "Thus the heavens and the earth *were finished,* and all the host of them. And on the seventh day

God *ended* his work which he had made [declared the work on which he was engaged finished]; and he rested on the seventh day from all his work which he had made." The NEB translates it: "On the sixth day God completed all the work he had been doing, and on the seventh day he ceased from all his work." The Septuagint expresses it, "And God *finished* on the sixth day his works which he made, and he ceased on the seventh day from all his works which he had made."

Thus the Bible believer learns two basic facts about the world of living things: (1) God by fiat created the basic types in the beginning, and (2) on Day Six God *concluded* His creation of basic types; therefore no addition of new basic kinds has occurred since Creation week through either spontaneous generation or macroevolution.

Through special revelation we learn that God performed a great work and that He ended that work. Since Creation week the earth's complement of basic types of plants and animals has not been augmented, but rather diminished through the extinction of certain forms which could not adjust to changed living conditions following Noah's Flood.

The present-day Bible-believing biologist is impressed most forcefully with the harmony which exists between the assertions of Genesis and the testimony of nature. Today we see the face of the earth teeming with a diversity of plants and animals. Structural similarities may appear in many groups, yet each basic kind stands as clearly cut as an island in an archipelago, with no connecting bridges.

This is the very picture given us at the close of Creation week. The land areas were verdant with plants in their basic kinds from the lowly carpeting forms to the lofty trees, from the redwood to the lichens on its bark and the herbaceous forms blossoming at its base. All kinds of animals swam in the waters, burrowed in the ground, crept, walked, and

THE FORM AND STRUCTURE OF LIVING THINGS 101

moved lightly over the land, climbed the trees, and flew through the air.

Organic diversity seemed the pattern of life, and yet throughout the whole of animate nature the phenomenon of discontinuity is clearly visible. Man, chimpanzees, cattle, horses, dogs, cats, pigeons, roses, water lilies, petunias, and sunflowers—each, in its respective kind, was strikingly discontinuous from all others. Evolutionists admit that because of this very discontinuity it is impossible to demonstrate macroevolution among living plants and animals. To find a demonstration of macroevolution they say one must go to the fossil record. Yet, as one studies the reports of finds, fossil paleontology repeatedly refutes this opinion.

The gaps between fossil groups of organisms are not a figment of wishful thinking on the part of the creationist. Rather, the paleontological record itself demonstrates fixity within the loci of basic types, with absence of intergrading forms or connecting links.

We recognize that this discontinuity among the fossils does not demonstrate special creation of basic types, but it does harmonize with such an origin. The evolutionists, on the other hand, are constantly required to exercise more and more faith in their theory as it becomes more obvious that intergrading forms necessary for macroevolution are absent in just those places where they are needed most to bolster the theory.

When evolutionists speak of discontinuity in the fossil record, they often say or infer that there are cases where connecting fossil links between basic types do exist. These bridges may be believed by faith, but they cannot be shown.

The *Archaeopteryx* is commonly given as the connecting link between birds and reptiles. Actually it would take many more forms than this one fossil curiosity to build the required bridge. The fact that the *Archaeopteryx* had some structures in common with both birds and reptiles does not necessarily mean more than does the fact that man has an eye similar to that of the squid and a humerus and radius and ulna in common with birds, whales, and bats.

Common origin indeed, but we would suggest that that origin was in the mind of one Creator with a master plan. Thus it is most likely that many supposed connecting links are, along with the groups they "connect," members of separately created basic types.

According to Genesis there was a unit in the living creation specified as the kind (Hebrew, *min*). As we have already noted, according to the record, the Creator commanded the earth to bring forth plants and animals; it was not as if He were casting a net into a murky, unknown sea, wondering what forms might appear when He drew in the net.

If an omniscient God first planned the basic kinds and then produced these very kinds, would He not have planned that they continue as enduring entities? It would be an astonishing thing if the Creator were to plan in great detail and produce all the variable basic forms, pronounce them "very good" (Genesis 1:31), and yet create them so that they would cross indiscriminately, erasing His handiwork as the generations passed.

What sort of entities were the original "kinds"? The precise technical Hebrew word *min,* kind, a singular collective, appears ten times in Genesis 1. In the remainder of the Old Testament it appears twenty-one times more.

In Leviticus 11, RSV, we find *min* applied respectively to the falcon, the raven, the hawk, the heron, the locust, the bald locust, the cricket, and the grasshopper. In Deuteronomy 14, RSV, it is applied to the raven, the ostrich, the nighthawk, the sea gull, the hawk, the little owl, the great owl, the water hen, the pelican, the vulture, the cormorant, the stork, and the heron.

THE FORM AND STRUCTURE OF LIVING THINGS 103

Although *min* is a somewhat imprecise word in Genesis 1, still in its use in its thirteen appearances in Leviticus and Deuteronomy it tends toward the *specific* rather than toward the general. It is never used so broadly as to suggest that the originally created kinds may have been groups as extensive and inclusive as to refer to the hairy, the scaly, or the feathered animals. At times it is used so specifically as to distinguish a "locust" from a "bald locust," a "little owl" from a "great owl." We may conclude therefore that no single category in modern taxonomy corresponds to the Genesis kind.

As we have noted above, the testimony of Genesis is that, with regard to the plants, "the earth brought forth vegetation, plants yielding seed according to their own kinds." Genesis 1:12, RSV. In other words, the distinguishing characteristic of the Genesis kind was more physiological (chemical, ie, potentially genetic) than morphological. The same was undoubtedly true of the animals.

After studying hybridization for years, I still suggest true fertilization as a test of the Genesis kind among sexually reproducing organisms. Plants and animals apparently have remained true to the law of their creation, and we still witness striking, clear-cut discontinuity.

During the Middle Ages schoolmen in church universities taught that according to Genesis no variation from generation to generation among plants and animals could occur. According to this scholastic view, reproduction was like the minting of coins—each coin a copy of the die that stamps it.

This narrow, extreme interpretation was still taught in Cambridge when Charles Darwin studied theology there in the late 1820s. Apparently Darwin left the interpretation of Genesis to the theology professors when he embarked on his five-year voyage around the world, 1831-36. He had believed that, according to Genesis, God had created plants and animals, and set them in the earth in the very forms of their 1831 appearance and location.

However, as Darwin studied the flora and fauna of islands and continents, he observed that not only had organisms moved over the earth, but they had also changed somewhat in their appearance. To illustrate, most of the islands of the Galápagos group were populated each with a different variety of tortoise and finch. The whole picture was not one of fixity as to location and form, but rather of migration with variation.

These observations troubled Darwin deeply; he thought they contradicted Genesis. After years of mental conflict he decided that Genesis must be wrong. In 1844, in a letter to his friend Joseph Dalton Hooker, a botanist, he wrote: "I have read heaps of agricultural and horticultural books and have never ceased collecting facts. At last gleams of light have come, and I am almost convinced (quite contrary to the opinion I started with) that species are not (it is like confessing a murder) immutable."[2]

Even in our day most people think Darwin disproved Genesis. Actually all he disproved was the schoolmen's *inaccurate interpretation* of Genesis. Tragically, Darwin failed to recognize that his observations were completely in harmony with Genesis.

With regard to the movement of animals over the earth after the great Flood, the Cambridge theologians seem to have missed Genesis 8:17, RSV: "Bring forth with you every living thing that is with you of all flesh—birds and animals and every creeping thing that creeps on the earth—that they may breed abundantly on the earth, and be fruitful and multiply upon the earth." The ark beached in the Near East, in "the mountains of Ararat" (Genesis 8:4), which would be in the general area of Armenia and eastern Turkey. In order to follow God's plan for them, the animals would have to

THE FORM AND STRUCTURE OF LIVING THINGS

migrate out from that center. The observations of keen-eyed Darwin which revealed *migration* with *variation* were according to God's plan revealed in Genesis, a plan that animals were to "breed abundantly on the earth" and "multiply upon the earth."

It is unfortunate that demonstrable variation has been named a microevolution, because this variation is not true evolution at all, as the term is commonly understood. Microevolution (variation) has never been shown to do more than produce a new breed, variety, species, or group of individuals, within a basic type *already on hand.* A cow may bring forth an Aberdeen-Angus, an Africander, an Ayrshire, a Brahman (Zebu), a Brown Swiss, a Devon, a Galloway, a Gaur, a Gayal, a Guernsey, a Hereford, a Holstein-Friesian, a Jersey, a Shorthorn, or even a Catalo. But this is only microevolution; all are merely breeds of the cow kind.

A fertilized corn ovule may develop into dent corn, flint corn, sweet corn, popcorn, starch corn, or pod corn and still accomplish only microevolution because these are still merely varieties of the corn kind. Microevolution may even go so far as to make a new species possible by selective breeding as demonstrated by Kozhevnikov,[3] or to change a race into a new biological species as explained by Dobzhansky.[4] As far as demonstrable evidence goes, no reproductive behavior of any type can accomplish macroevolution.

A common practice of evolutionists is to marshal many illustrations of microevolution and represent that all this process needs to accomplish macroevolution is enough time. This assumption can never be shown to be true, because one of the most completely demonstrated principles of biology is that all processes of variation among plants and animals can do no more than produce another variant within a basic type *already in existence.*

This extremely basic and important principle has been overlooked by biologists because of their obsession with macroevolution. The caution by the English evolutionist G. A. Kerkut is apropos here: "It might be suggested that if it is possible to show that the present-day forms are changing and evolution [microevolution] is occurring at this level, why can't one extrapolate and say that this in effect has led to the changes we have seen right from the viruses to the mammals? Of course one can say that the small observable changes in modern species may be the sort of things that lead to all the major changes, but what right have we to make such an extrapolation? We may feel that this is the answer to the problem, but is it a satisfactory answer? A blind acceptance of such a view may in fact be the closing of our eyes to as yet undiscovered factors which may remain undiscovered for many years if we believe that the answer has been found."[5]

The great majority of evolutionists do accept their developmental theory blindly. With most it has been a matter of following a leader. And now, having committed themselves for evolution, they lose the power for open-minded study in a smog of dogmatism. A famous evolutionist geneticist once wrote me that he was not opposed to the idea of God at work in nature, but because "things in nature are *as if* evolution were a fact," any other view of origins than that of evolution would to him be blasphemy. An obsession does great things to a person. With Napoleon it caused him to declare, "There are no Alps!" With the evolutionist it blinds him to the testimony of nature, though he is familiar with it.

As an aside, it may come as a startling anomaly to a Bible-believing scientist to hear the opinion that acceptance of the Genesis account of special creation is a blasphemous act. In the production of basic types, the Creator cannot be charged with trickery for two reasons: (1) Careful study of living things (and their fossil ancestors) shows no real evidence for organic evolution. (2) Even if it were assumed that nature gave an appearance of organic evolution, man would have no excuse to imagine such an origin, because God states clearly in the Guidebook (the Bible) that all basic types came into being by special creation.

Two influential books in recent years have been the beautifully illustrated Life Nature Library volume *Evolution*, by Ruth Moore and the editors of *Life*, and the even more handsome volume *Atlas of Evolution*, by Sir Gavin de Beer.[6] *The impressive evidence which fills these volumes is for microevolution only!*

The script which directs the mind to macroevolution is purely philosophical. If you will *believe* that the narrator is telling the truth, you can become an evolutionist. It will have to be an act of faith, because every example given demonstrates the biological truth that all variation, naturally or artificially produced, can develop *nothing basically new*.

What is the significance of similar form and structure? Does it indicate genetic relationship? Not necessarily; there is an alternate view. Creationists see in this a work of special creation of basic types originated in the mind and by the command of the same Creator.

Interestingly, both creationist and evolutionist begin by acknowledging the truism in biology that "like produces like." *Both* would be flabbergasted if a sparrow were to produce a warbler, or if a rose produced a geranium. Reproductive isolation, even among sympatric kinds, is the natural way of life.

Nevertheless the evolutionist pushes on past natural fact and insists that macroevolution is a logical extension of the self-evident facts—that structural resemblance signifies genetic relationship; that the degree of closeness of structural resemblance generally runs parallel with closeness of kinship. The evolutionist realizes that if he cannot rely upon this assumption garnered from comparative anatomy, (a concept now quite generally discredited), he cannot attempt to validate the concept of evolution. The developmentalist as well as the creationist relies upon the fact of heredity in everyday life. He plants a certain kind of seed and expects to get a certain plant. When breeding a certain kind of dog, he expects offspring of the same breed. The production of like by like is natural law. Yet evolution builds upon the unnatural assumption that, at many times in the past, basic kinds *have* produced something basically new. That is the only way new basic kinds could arise, and yet nature has no mechanism to perform such unnatural acts.

Informed scientists know that production of a new basic kind of plant or animal may be a *logical* extension of a truism in biology, but it is not *biological.* Thus the evolutionist theorizes from simple to complex by recourse to assumed unnatural and apparently impossible behavior, while the creationist sees the basic types taking form through the supernatural acts of a transcendent Being. The very real discontinuity in nature supports only the view of the creationist.

Do form and structure furnish a key to membership in Genesis kinds? No closer kinship can be imagined than that which exists between identical human twins. Careful statistical studies to determine the exact degree of their resemblances to one another have been made on over two hundred sets (see Newman[7]), revealing the rather startling fact that on the average they showed a 93 percent identical coefficient of correlation. The only structural resemblance belonging to this order of closeness is that existing between right and left halves (ie, antimeric) of a single individual, such as the two sides of the face, or the two hands.

THE FORM AND STRUCTURE OF LIVING THINGS

The next degree of resemblance is between a brother and his sister, who are about 50 percent identical. Cousins of various grades have proportionately lower degrees of resemblance, in keeping with their degree of kinship. Thus it may be expected that among the descendants of any original kind, similarity of form and structure to the extent of distinguishing a cow kind of animal from a horse kind, for example, will certainly exist.

How can we distinguish a horse from a cow? The evolutionist and the creationist both resort to a cluster of bodily characteristics as distinguishing marks of membership in these respective kinds.

According to Genesis, resemblances among members of the bovine kind may indicate blood relationship, but resemblances between members of the bovine kind and the equine kind, for instance, do not indicate genetic continuity between them. The evolutionist, employing in a broad way what he calls the principle of homology, takes "a short step in logic"[8] beyond actual performance in nature and assumes that two somewhat similar basic kinds have been derived one from the other or both from a common ancestral form.

It is explained to us that it is *logically* impossible to draw the line at any level of organic classification and say that structural resemblance is the product of heredity up to such and such a level but that beyond this arbitrarily chosen point heredity ceases to operate. It would be wise to introduce this statement by saying, "*To the evolutionist* it seems logically impossible—" Human logic is possibly imperfect, and the facts of origins may not coincide with it. To the creationist it is at least equally reasonable that the Creator could form a man and a chimpanzee anatomically in a similar way without having to derive them from a common stem ancestor.

The creationist notes carefully that the evolutionist attempts in some cases to argue that resemblance indicates genetic relationship, while in other cases it does not—for example in the area of homologous structures, analogous structures, convergence or parallelism of form, and adaptive radiation.

Evolutionists define *homologous structures* as those similar in anatomical detail and in their mode of embryonic origin, irrespective of whether they perform the same functions. Of course homologous structures are demonstrable and are as real to the creationist as to the evolutionist. However, evolutionists' conclusion that homologous structures represent the same hereditary units, and have been derived from the same or similar ancestors, is pure speculation. Because in principle it is contrary to Genesis, creationists reject it. To them, such structures reveal the ingenuity of the Creator in adapting the same basic anatomical pattern to different uses.

Structures which are superficially alike in form or in function, usually in both, though anatomically quite different, are said by the evolutionist to be *analogous*. Thus the wings of the bird and of a bee are said to be analogous. The same is true of the human lung and the gill of a fish. These structures can be shown in the laboratory to be entirely different in their embryonic derivation. *Convergence* or *parallelism of form* is thought by the progressionist to be the result of adaptation to similar conditions of life. Additional examples are the three aquatic vertebrates: the shark, the ichthyosaur, and the porpoise. All of these have the same fusiform body, median, paired, and caudal fins, and all swim (or swam) in the same way.

Because one is a fish, one a reptile, and one a mammal, the evolutionist holds that they do not have the same genetic continuity. In such examples the evolutionist sees what he thinks are strong evidences of descent with modification,

THE FORM AND STRUCTURE OF LIVING THINGS 111

while the creationist is delighted with the ingenuity of the Creator in adapting different animals to the same specific environment.

Creationists and evolutionists should be pleased whenever they can agree upon the same interpretation of certain natural facts. The phenomenon of analogous structures is one of these uncommon instances. Both agree that structural resemblance of this type does not indicate genetic relationship even though superficially they are quite similar. Because of this superficial resemblance, evolutionists refer to such cases as illustrating, in H. F. Osborn's words, "the law of convergence or parallelism of form."[9] The thought is that these different lines of organisms have gradually adapted themselves through time to the same environment until they have finally reached a stage of physical resemblance which might seem to indicate genetic relationship—an interestingly different conclusion from that reached by evolutionists regarding homologous structures.

Additional examples of *"convergence"* are the fact that running animals generally have long legs and a tendency to stand on the toes. The toes may be reduced; the horse has only one. Climbing animals possess clinging appendages, structures such as hooked claws, prehensile fingers or tail, suction pads on the feet, and similar adaptations. Burrowing animals usually have an extraheavy shoulder girdle and strong forelimbs with heavy gouging claws.

The evolutionist agrees that such resemblances indicate no blood relationship within each ecological group, but he still pleads for evolution: "Analogous structures, while not considered as evidences of kinship, are strong evidences of descent with modification, for their very existence implies that they have changed from a former condition to one in which they are adapted to a new medium."[10] This illustrates what imaginative interpretation can do with demonstrated facts.

In the matter of *adaptive radiation* there is always the problem of just how far it can be demonstrated in nature. The creationist accepts demonstrated facts, but in this area where does demonstration end and speculation begin? Often we see in organisms a remarkable capacity for individual adjustment to special conditions. Not only may the organism be amazingly well fitted for the average conditions of its environment, but, likewise, it may be able to adjust itself to relatively wide variations from the optimum condition.

In making these adjustments the organism may respond with changes in its physical body, such as assuming white pelage in winter, or growing a thick, rough coat of long hair in cold weather and a short-haired, smooth coat in summer. Or some plants will grow entire leaves when well-watered and develop only spines when growing under dry conditions, as in the English gorse.

Thus to a certain point adaptive radiation may occur. Possibly Darwin's finches on the Galápagos Islands are an actual case of such radiation in which one kind of bird has become adapted to special environmental factors, until its variants came to occupy all the ecological habitats of the islands from ground to tree, and eating both plant food and insects.

But we must remember that adaptive radiation has not been demonstrated to produce more than variants within their respective kinds. These birds that Darwin studied on the Galápagos, whether eating cactus seeds on the ground or pursuing worms in a tree limb with a cactus thorn,[11] had accomplished nothing more than new variants of Darwin's finches—new species, genera, and subfamily, but no new basic type.

THE FORM AND STRUCTURE OF LIVING THINGS

The facts do not support the idea that because all tetrapods (land vertebrates except snakes) have the same three bones in their forelimbs they must have experienced adaptive radiation into their present form and structure from a primitive form by changes in proportion, fusion of parts, or loss of parts.

All *primary* adaptations, such as fitness of fish for the aquatic environment, and the squirrel for the arboreal environment, were made in the beginning. Secondary adaptations, more or less minor adjustments since Creation, accomplish only new varieties in basic kinds already in existence.

That the area of comparative anatomy is declared by evolutionists to be "one of the most important fields of evidence for evolution"[12] is actually no recommendation for evolutionism. That necessary "short step in logic" which could produce morphological changes resulting in new basic types—this "short step" carries macroevolution out of reality into the world of make-believe.

The problem of classification of plants and animals still stands as a challenge to the biologist. References to this science appear frequently in a discussion of form and structure, because they constitute the basis for all classification systems attempted so far. The father of modern taxonomy, the creationist Carolus Linnaeus, during the most active period of his life, *assumed* that the groups he called species were the created units, and for convenience in his work with plants he used the sexual parts of flowers in a purely artificial classification system.

He experimented with maplike diagrams, but he found that no arrangement he could make would always place similar forms together and separate dissimilar forms. For this reason such diagrams never gained much popularity as summaries of taxonomic data.

In their pursuit of a means of expressing their findings diagrammatically, taxonomists next tried to arrange living forms on a ladderlike figure—a ladder which attempted to include everything from amoebae to archangels. This was based on the *assumption* that adaptation of living things is progressive—any animal should be preceded by one somewhat lower in the scale of life and followed by one higher in this scale. This worked fairly well for the fishes, the amphibians, and the reptiles.

However, the series cannot continue on with birds and mammals because the majority of birds are in every respect quite as "high" as the majority of mammals, thus requiring two rungs at the same level of the ladder. This type of dilemma is repeated frequently not only among higher forms, but even more frequently in the lower levels of classification.

This need for parallel rungs at many levels soon suggested a third type of diagram, one in the form of a tree. This invention delighted evolutionists, because they *conceived* that, as in the case of the tree, a development of organisms had occurred from one or a very few simple sources, the growth being accompanied by branching and differentiation.

However, they recognized that unlike the growth of a tree, the processes of branching and differentiation could not be directly observed. Faith and imagination had to supply all of the phylogenetic tree except its branches and twigs. For that reason the evolutionists' tree of life is really a curiosity, or even a monstrosity. The real basic types appear on this "tree" with no genuine, demonstrable connection or support.

Developmentalists are confused when they try to attach the real branches at the proper branch or on the trunk. The creationist would suggest that they drop this losing game

THE FORM AND STRUCTURE OF LIVING THINGS

and place a Creator as the "trunk" of their tree of life as the originator of all basic types.

Discontinuity in the world of living things dooms the evolutionists' tree of life, at least in the sense that all the basic kinds have developed from a distant common ancestor and are therefore genetically related. The field for the development of a classification system based upon the truth of Genesis is still wide open.

Creationists do not speak of *one* phylogenetic tree, but they do consider a whole forest of smaller or simpler trees. Each tree would represent one basic type; and in some cases, as clusters of forms whose individuals will hybridize are studied, a considerable tree appears. The cabbage, for instance, apparently may have varied so widely within its basic type as to shape into a very intriguing tree. The same is true more or less with most of our domesticated plants and animals. What a delightful complexity if we were to unravel the true phylogenetic tree of even *one* of our choice roses!

A discussion of comparative anatomy from the point of view of the special creationist would be seriously lacking if Linnaeus's theory of *archetypes* were not mentioned. "Archetype," synonymous with *prototype,* springs from the Latin *archetypum,* an original pattern from which an object is formed.

Linnaeus's theory of archetypes assumed that the Creator worked from a series of plans, the archetypes, limited in number. These archetypes fell into clear-cut categories. In his system of classification he recognized only classes, orders, genera, and species. The class would correspond to a major archetype, while the various orders within a class would be lesser archetypes, and so on down the hierarchy.

This theory seems reasonable yet one which, if employed by the Creator, was by no means used in every case. Among mammals it is possible to explain that often both males and females have nipples because of a creation which employed archetypes.

Speculation takes over when we study such instances as the fact that although the dandelion produces abundance of pollen, still this pollen is sterile. Is this due to the Creator's adherence to a plan which required that certain flowers shall have both stamens and pistils even if the anthers produce only inviable pollen? Or has mutational change occurred here since Creation?

In the case of certain blind cave fishes, creationist Louis Agassiz believed that the Creator had created them blind and placed them in caves in that condition where we find them today.[13] In that case the nonfunctional optic nerves present in certain of these fish (*Amblyopsis, Typhlichthys,* and *Troglicthys*[14]) would be mere extraneous structures due to the Creator's adherence to a type which required optic nerves. Or is it not more likely that in such instances the eyes, including the distal portions of the optic nerves, have suffered from mutation at some time since Creation?

When pondering archetypes, we must take care not to fall into a dogmatic position. Evolutionists have affirmed that if special creation occurred, then the Creator *must* have used archetypes throughout; and if He employed such models, then He would be obliged to use them *in every pertinent case.* Man should be cautious in conjuring up supposed courses of procedure which he assumes a Creator would be required to follow if basic types arose by special creation. This evolutionist activity consists of putting up straw men and then gleefully knocking them down. What omniscient Creator would guarantee to follow certain methods and reject others as specified by His creatures?

In our study of comparative anatomy we find instances where the Creator appears to have employed archetypes rather broadly. But at the same time we discover another

THE FORM AND STRUCTURE OF LIVING THINGS 117

creature's surprise use of some other form or structure for the same purpose. The different structure appears to exist only to introduce variety.

The Creator employed many ways of providing motion for animals: moving in water, locomoting over dry surfaces, moving freely through the trees, and flying through the air. General plans such as archetypes present a restful, stabilizing organization in nature; but at the same time the variations which appear at every hand add a zest to nature study which avoids tedium. The more one familiarizes himself with the structural forms of plants and animals, the nearer he concludes that the Creator delights in variation. Creation of man in the image of God seems to include an endowment with the capacity of thoroughly enjoying this delightful diversity supplied so bountifully in the form and structure of living things.

CHAPTER 10

Thoughts to Ponder

Among the important items a student of origins should ponder are the following:

1. There is no absolute laboratory proof for the manner of origin of living things. The pertinent evidence is not coercive or compulsive, but subjective, circumstantial, and persuasive. The student must make his own decision as to what he will believe about origins.

2. There are two principal theories (actually hypotheses or doctrines) of origins: (a) special creation, and (b) organic evolution. Each view has many variations.

3. The doctrine of special creation teaches that God created all basic types of organisms. This great event is generally conceived of as having occurred only a few thousand years ago.

4. The doctrine of organic evolution teaches that all life on this earth has developed from one or a few one-celled organisms. Complex and specialized forms gradually evolved from the simple and generalized. This first life is generally believed to have appeared some 600 million years ago, possibly billions of years.

5. According to the creationist view, there is no genetic relationship between any of the basic types, while the evolutionist view holds that all living things may be genetically related.

THOUGHTS TO PONDER

6. Both creationists and evolutionists claim to accept all demonstrable natural facts.

7. Natural science consists first of *demonstrable facts*, and second of a *speculative portion* in which an explanation or rationalization of the demonstrable phenomena is sought.

As an illustration of the two phases of natural science, let us take a problem involving the bones of the forelimbs of vertebrates. Let us clean the bones of a forelimb of a horse, a cow, a dog, a cat, a man, an ape, a bird, a bat, and a whale. With these bones laid out on a table, we proceed to study them. This study discloses that the forelimbs of these vertebrates have the same three bones: the humerus, the radius, and the ulna.

Having thus certified the presence of the same three bones in all these vertebrate limbs, we have reached the end of demonstrable science. We are now ready to enter the second phase of science, the speculative.

We sit down with the bones before us and ponder the meaning of their similarity. Finally two hypotheses are reached: (1) the evolutionist says, Here is proof that all these animals had a common ancestor; therefore evolution must have occurred. (2) The creationist says, Here is confirmation of Genesis—one Creator with a master plan. Which hypothesis is correct? Your answer here will depend upon where you wish to place your faith. The careful student must always distinguish which material in science is *demonstrable* and which is merely *speculative* and respect the other man's right to make his own decision.

8. *Microevolution,* as defined by creationists, is the term used to indicate the development of new variants *within* a basic type, ie, the development of new breeds or races, subspecies, species, subgenera, genera, subfamilies, and possibly even families, so long as these are populations of

individuals which obviously (morphologically) belong to the same basic type. Defined in this way, microevolution is a demonstrable phenomenon recognized by both creationists and evolutionists.

Probably one of the best collections of illustrations of microevolution among mammals is found in the Russian zoologist A. V. Yablokov's book (1974) *Variability of Mammals*[1]. Since Darwin, a great deal of study has been done, and is being done, on what Yablokov calls "intrapopulation somatic or phenotypic variation." This is change which is constantly occurring within a single population and can be illustrated by variability of length and thickness of hair in the aquatic rodent coypu (*Myocaster coypus*); by variability in white spots on the tails, and in the body weight and length of the mouse *Peromyscus maniculatus*; by variability of the number of skin plates of the nine-banded armadillo (*Dasypus novemcinctus*); by variability of the number of caudal and thoracic vertebrae in the common seal (*Phoca vitulina*); by variability of the weight of the thyroid gland in the kangaroo (*Neomys fodiens*); and so on.

Yablokov has helped greatly in filling the real need to bring together the increasingly abundant data on microevolution in mammals, and to organize them into a consistent body. His book, together with the published symposium of the Zoological Society of London on variation in mammals (1970) by R. J. Berry and H. N. Southern (editors), entitled *Variation in Mammalian Populations*,[2] brings to us the most up-to-date information on what variation is accomplishing among hairy animals (mammals). Most impressively, all that this demonstrated change within any population of mammals can do is to produce variants which are unquestionably still members of their own respective peculiar basic type. That is to say, apparently no natural process, or processes, of change exist which can produce even one

THOUGHTS TO PONDER

new basic type of organism.

9. Macroevolution (or *megaevolution*) to the creationist is the term used to indicate an undemonstrable hypothesis for the development of a new basic type from a different one. Defined in this way, it belongs to speculative science. It concerns the origin of new basic types or kinds—not just species. Evolutionists have confused the issue of origins here by using this term not only to indicate an assumed origin of new basic types in geologic time, but also to include so trivial a thing as the origin of a new variant within an existing basic type in present time.

10. No empirical (laboratory) evidence substantiates that true connecting links between basic types ever existed. Among both living forms and fossil forms a clear-cut discontinuity is universally present. If a true, graded series does or did exist between two basic types, then the two types probably are, or were, merely variants, races, possibly, of a single polytypic species. Such graded series, "links," could never accomplish macroevolution.

11. The actual, observable, clear-cut discontinuity which exists in living and fossil nature constitutes the greatest single roadblock on the highway to organic evolution.

12. The *demonstrable* facts fit harmoniously into the doctrine of special creation. The more that is learned about variation, the greater the harmony between demonstrable facts and special creation.

13. The concept of evolution rests upon the assumption that basic types have produced new basic types. The evolutionist argues that only "a short step in logic" is necessary to bridge between actual performance in nature and macroevolution. The student of origins must remember that, although this step *may be logical, it is not biological.* No bona fide instance has ever been recorded where one basic type produced a new basic type. From the beginning

of empirical science to our day we have had sufficient opportunity to learn that *time alone* does not and cannot cause a change of function in natural processes.

14. Through the eyes of a classificationist, only two clearly observable entities exist in the living world: (1) the individual, and (2) the basic type. The taxonomic categories of biologists are quite arbitrary. Specialists in this branch of biology differ in their views on this. Battles have been fought over the proper use of the term "species," battles which could have been prevented if taxonomists had focused their observation upon a higher level than that of the individual.

15. Special creation teaches that originally created kinds are distinguishable today in two ways: (1) by the closely similar morphological characters of members of a basic kind, and (2) by *true fertilization* when eggs and sperms are brought together. In every known instance where true fertilization occurs, the mates are sufficiently similar in appearance to indicate membership in the same basic kind.

16. Because no modern taxonomic categories, not even the biological nor polytypic species, appear to be equivalent in all cases to the Genesis kind, I suggested in 1941 the use of *baramin (bara,* created, and *min,* kind—plural *baramins)* as a name for the present-day Genesis kind, ie, the basic type or kind. George McCready Price and Harold W. Clark used the terms "type form" and "created type" in reference to the created units, but not in so close a definition as the *baramin,* a unit assumed to be discoverable through laboratory procedure. Recently, unaware of my earlier proposal of the name *baramin* for the modern descendants of the Genesis kind, Hilbert R. Siegler[3] has suggested the name *genus* for the same identical natural group. The detailed agreement of these two biologists with regard to the present-day distinguishing features of the descendants of the original basic groups is most significant.

THOUGHTS TO PONDER

17. One of the most basic and well-demonstrated of biological principles is that of the *limitation of variation*. This means the production of no more than additional variants within a basic type already in existence. Because of a universal obsession by a hypothesis of origins, to the great loss of biological science, this tremendously important principle has not been recognized by evolutionist biologists.

18. The Bible knows nothing about organic evolution. It regards the origin of man by special creation as a historical fact. Notice the attitude of Christ toward the Genesis account of origins. Matthew 19:4-6. He accepted the details of Genesis 1 and 2, and chapter 5, verses 1 and 2, as true history. The evolutionist, whether atheistic, deistic, theistic, or agnostic, holds that man has risen through the animals.

19. In view of the subjectivity of the evidence upon which a decision on the matter of origins must be made, creationism and evolutionism should be respected as alternate viewpoints.

GLOSSARY

acquired characteristics. Superficial alteration of a living creature; for example, loss of an eye or a foot by accident; or stunted growth of a spruce tree at timberline because of severe environmental factors. No one has ever demonstrated the inheritance of an acquired characteristic. Such inheritance was disproved by Weismann, who cut off the tails of twenty-two generations of mice and found that the tails of their descendants were no shorter than those of a similar group whose tails had not been cut off.

adaptive radiation. The filling of the various habitats in an isolated area by related animals of a single stock. The isolation of a group in one habitat on an island, for example, from those in surrounding habitats on the same island may permit variation to result in limited differences in form and structure. This possibly is illustrated by Darwin's finches on the Galápagos Islands where, largely through the development of differences in size and shape of the bill, these related finches can do the work done in other areas by woodpeckers, warblers, and various plant eaters. In areas open to all types of birds, these specialized forms might not be able to compete successfully and thus be subjected to progressive extinction with accompanying elimination of evidences of adaptive radiation.

allopolyploid. The term *polyploidy* is applied to instances, usually in plants, where in each cell of the plant the whole set of chromosomes has been duplicated one or more times. If this duplication has occurred in the cells of a hybrid between two different species or two genera, the resulting individuals are called allopolyploids.

analogous structures. Body parts which have similar functions in two different animals although they may be different in structure. For example, a lung and a fish gill, though quite different in structure, are used for the same purpose (respiration) and thus are analogous.

annelids. Segmented worms such as earthworms, marine worms, and leeches.

antediluvian. Before Noah's Flood. In the Scriptures this would refer to time from Creation week (Genesis 1, 2) to Noah's Flood (Genesis 6 to 8).

anthropomorphic. Concept of God under a human form, or with human attributes and affections.

apologist. One who speaks or writes in defense of a faith.

apomixis. The process of increase of individuals among plants without any form of sexual union. Parthenogenesis and apogamy are forms of apomixis. The general term applied to these organisms is *apomicts*. In apomixis there is no fertilization. It has not been found in self-fertilized plants.

arboreal. Of or pertaining to a tree or trees.

Archaeopteryx. A genus of reptilelike fossil bird found only in the upper Jurassic of Europe.

archetype. Original pattern or model from which a thing is made or formed.

artificial insemination. Introduction of male germ cells into the female reproductive tract by other than the natural method.

asexual. Having no sex. Reproduction by spores, root sprouts, runners, rhizomes, gemmae, tubers, corms, bulbs, or cuttings and buds.

autopolyploid. See "allopolyploid." If a duplication of the chromosome complement has occurred within each of two parents in a *single species,* the next generation is called an autopolyploid. Autopolyploids will have four identical chromosomes of each kind. As noted above, allopolyploids occur when a hybrid is formed between *two species* or *two genera* in which a doubling of the chromosome sets has occurred in the germ cells of the parents before fertilization of the egg.

bara. Hebrew verb meaning "created".

baramin. A coined word formed by uniting the Hebrew roots *bara* (created) and *min* (kind). "Baramin" is suggested as a modern name for the created units, the *kinds* referred to in Genesis 1 and 2.

GLOSSARY

basic type. An expression used in this book to indicate stable populations in nature such as cows, horses, cats, dogs, men, oaks, maples, wheat, and roses.

biological species. A plant or animal population consisting of individuals which do or can cross and produce fertile offspring.

blastomeres. The cells formed by the early cell divisions of the fertilized egg.

brachiopods. Marine animals of the Phylum *Brachiopoda* which live in a limy bivalve shell whose halves are dorsal and ventral.

bryophytes. Plants of the Phylum *Bryophyta* containing the mosses and liverworts.

Cambrian period. Commonly thought of by geologists as the bottom fossil-bearing layer or stratum of rock.

category. A class to which a certain assertion applies; a class or division formed by the nature of the consideration entertained or for the purposes of a given discussion or classification, as species, genus, family, class, order, and phylum are biological categories, listed here in order from the smallest group of individuals to the largest.

chromosome. The structure in the nucleus of a cell which carries the genes and hence determines heredity. Chromosomes are commonly rod-shaped and become visible only in a dividing cell.

chromosome aberrations. Group name for variation in numbers of chromosomes and for rearrangements of chromosomal material.

chromosome complement. The whole collection of chromosomes in a cell nucleus.

class. See "classification categories" below used in naming organisms.

classification. The systematic arrangement (or method of arrangement) of animals and plants in groups (categories) according to some definite plan or sequence. Classification is necessary because of the sheer numbers of species, even if no other purpose beyond that of facilitating study were served.

classification categories. From the standpoint of number of individuals which these main subdivisions represent, arranged from highest number to lowest number, we have this sequence: phylum, class, order, family, genus, and species.

classificationist, classifier. One who names (classifies) animals or plants.

comparative anatomy. As the term infers, this is the study to determine similarities and differences of the same organ or organ system in a single phylum, or it may also be a comparative study of the same system among several phyla.

convergence of form. The appearance of similar structures in what the evolutionist calls "unrelated forms," such as the eyes of vertebrates which are almost identical with those of the squid.

creation, creationism, creationists. The point of view of origins (all doctrines of origins are undemonstrable) which teaches that an omniscient, omnipotent, transcendent Creator spoke all basic types of plants and animals into existence. There are two kinds of creationists:

1. *Special creationists:* Creationists who believe in a literal Genesis and understand that the days of Creation week were 24-hour days; and that Creation week took place only some 6000 years ago.

2. *Progressive creationists:* Creationists who accept the evolutionist's geological timetable and hold that God specially created the basic types of organisms, progressing from simple to complex, over a period of at least 600 million years, thus considering that the "days" of Creation week may have been geological periods of millions of years. Some progressive creationists believe that finally when man was created, God, over a period of six literal days, revealed to him what He (God) had been creating during the preceding 600 million years. Neither view recognizes genetic relationship between basic types.

crossability. Ability to breed with other individuals, species, and genera of the same basic kind.

crossbreeding. Mating of two varieties or breeds of the same species.

crustacean. Animal possessed of gills, a chitinous limy exoskeleton, two pairs of antennae, and with the first two body regions (head and thorax) commonly fused into one. Examples: crayfish, water fleas, crabs, barnacles, and sow bugs.

deletion (genetic). Breaking away and loss of a portion of a chromosome.

developmentalist. One who believes in organic evolution (macroevolution).

diploid. A chromosome complement which is made up of two of each kind of chromosome.

GLOSSARY

discontinuity (biological). It is an observable fact that variation in nature produces no kind of continuous distribution. The living world is not an array of individuals in which any two variants are connected by unbroken series of intergrades. Instead, living things form separate, discrete clusters. Each cluster consists of individuals possessing some common characteristics and focusing on a modal point in their variations. This existence of all living things in these discrete clusters is called organic or biological discontinuity, or discontinuity of organic variation.

discrete. Separate, individually distinct.

DNA. Deoxyribonucleic acid, the nucleic acid now thought to constitute the heritable (genetic) material in both higher and lower organisms, except where ribonucleic acid may perform this function in certain viruses.

dominant. A gene which expresses itself even when present in a single dose.

duplications. Additions of one or more genes, as a result of which the organism carries the same gene repeated in its haploid chromosome complement.

echinoderms. Marine animals with radiate symmetry in adults. Examples: Sea lilies, starfish, brittle stars, sea urchins, and sea cucumbers.

ecological varieties (races). Often these cannot be distinguished from geographical races. However, not uncommonly in the same geographical area one may find races or varieties of crayfish, some requiring brackish water and some living in fresh springwater. Races of mosquitoes may exist in the same area and yet never meet because they show different preferences for altitude, relative humidity, or temperature. These are properly ecological varieties or races.

effulgence. Radiant splendor; brilliance.

empirical science. Founded upon experiment or experience alone.

endemic. Native in, living naturally in, or confined to a specific area.

evolution, evolutionism, and evolutionists. Evolutionism is the undemonstrable doctrine of origin of living things, which teaches that the first life appeared on this earth in what are described as simple, single-celled blobs. These, it is assumed, gave rise to more complicated masses of cells, and so on, until the most complex living things were finally developed. There are various kinds of evolutionists; for example:

1. *Agnostic:* Believes that not enough evidence is available to suggest how life appeared on this earth or how the kinds of plants and animals came into being; yet he holds that the complex forms evolved from the simple.

2. *Atheistic:* Also called *mechanistic.* Believes that there is no higher power in the universe than natural processes; organisms appeared and developed by chance.

3. *Deistic:* Believes that a personal God set up the natural physical world and then created a simple form of life from which all other forms eventually evolved. After invoking a God to form the first life supernaturally, he then follows the thinking of the mechanistic evolutionist.

4. *Theistic:* Believes that God does exist and that He created all things and sustains them moment by moment. However, the theistic evolutionist assumes that God evolved the more complex and specialized from the more simple so that all living forms are genetically related.

family. See "classification categories."

fertilization (true). Occurs when the nuclei of the egg and the sperm, each with its full haploid complement of chromosomes, fuse to form the single zygote cell, and all the chromosomes of the two gametes appear in the equatorial plane of the zygote in preparation for the formation of the first two blastomeres of the embryo. If the chromosomes of the sperm do not join in the formation of the first two blastomeres, then true fertilization has not occurred.

fixity (of creation). All empirical evidence indicates that each basic type was created in such a way as to be unable to produce a new basic type. For example, all true cattle were fixed or limited chemically at Creation in such a way that they can, upon reproduction, produce only additional cattle.

gastrula stage. A stage in embryonic development in which the embryo consists of an outer and an inner layer of cells enclosing a cavity and having an opening at one end.

gene. A unit of heredity consisting of a sequence of nucleotides which has as its function the manufacture of one of the many proteins which result in the differences we observe among living things. The name "gene" is synonymous with DNA and is, chemically speaking, a molecule of deoxyribonucleic acid.

GLOSSARY

gene mutation. A chemical change in a gene. Levine describes it as "a change that has occurred at the level of one to a few nucleotides within the DNA molecule and below the resolution of the electron microscope."

gene pool. The sum total of all the hereditary factors (the genes, the DNA) in a single population in which all individuals can breed freely among themselves.

Genesis kind. In Genesis 1 and 2 we read that on Days Three, Five, and Six of Creation week, God created the basic kinds of plants and animals. These basic units among living things are referred to by creationists as "Genesis kinds."

genetic relationship (often popularly called "blood relationship"). To be related genetically is to have a common inheritance such as exists among all members of a family tree.

genotype. Classification made on the basis of genetic formulae (the genes present).

geographic varieties. Interfertile populations of a single kind which apparently have separated by migration accompanied by the development of minor variations. An illustration is found in the more than thirty subspecies of the song sparrow distributed across North America and up the west coast of Canada.

genus. See "classification categories."

haploid. The chromosome count when one member of each chromosome pair is present in a cell. This situation exists in mature germ cells (eggs and sperms).

heteroploidy. The loss of one chromosome from a set, or the addition of one or more chromosomes to one set, or the loss of both chromosomes of a pair.

hexaploid. An organism in which each cell has six times the basic chromosome number.

homologous structures. Organs that are usually similar in structure and always the same in embryological development (origin). Homologous organs may have similar functions, as the legs of a man and the hind legs of a dog; or they may have different functions, as, for example, the arms of a man and the wings of a bird.

Hottentot. A South African race apparently allied to both the Bushmen and Bantus, and possibly originating from an ancient cross of these two.

hybrid. The offspring of the union of a male of one breed, variety, race, species, genus, etc., with the female of another. The cross may be as near as a white guinea pig with a black one, or one breed of dent corn with another dent breed, or as wide as the cross of a horse with an ass, or of a radish with a cabbage.

hybridization. Act or process of producing hybrids.

hypothesis (working). A tentative theory or supposition provisionally adopted to explain certain facts and to guide in the investigation of others.

insemination (artificial). The placement, with the aid of laboratory equipment, of male sex cells (in semen) in the reproductive tract of the female.

interfertile species. Species which can cross and produce fertile offspring.

interspecific variation (macroevolution). Variation *assumed* to be of such magnitude and quality as to result in the eventual production of a new basic type. New biological *species* result from *variation*, but no new basic types have ever been known to result from macroevolution.

intraspecific variation (microevolution). Variation within a species which may be due to hereditary factors or to nongenetic modification of the appearance caused by local environmental conditions. Some groups of animals seem particularly subject to such modification. For example, in freshwater bivalves (*Anodonta*, "clams") and freshwater snails, more than 250 described "species" of *Anodonta* are merely local variants of a single species, and in the pond snails of the genus *Lymnaea*, more than 1000 names have been reduced to about forty species. This kind of variation, by definition, never does more than produce new variants within the species.

intratypal species. Species which apparently have developed within a single basic type or kind.

inversion. Within a single chromosome, a block of genes may rotate by 180 degrees. For example, a chromosome with genes in the order ABCDEFG may change to ABEDCFG.

Jordanian species. Populations to which species names have been assigned although the groups may obviously be no more than subspecies or even mere races or varieties. Because the French botanist Jordan (early 1800s) was among the first to follow this practice, such "species" have been called "Jordanian." Taxonomists who follow Jordan in assignment of species names are sometimes called "splitters."

GLOSSARY   133

law of convergence or, not of parallelism of form. Reference is made here to the fact of occurrence of structures in animals, which structures are superficially alike in form or in function, usually in both, though anatomically quite different. Such forms are called "analagous" by the evolutionist. Creationists and evolutionists agree that structural resemblance of this type does not indicate blood relationship even though superficially they are quite similar. To the evolutionist these different lines of organisms have gradually adapted themselves through time to the same environment until they have finally reached a stage of physical resemblance. To the creationist these animals were in the beginning created in these forms which fit them for their respective environments.

lethal factors or genes. A gene which, when present in the cells of an individual in both members of a chromosome pair, produces death. Such factors have been found in every kind of plant and animal that has been studied genetically.

Linnaean species. Broad species which include all individuals that are fertile among themselves. In Linnaeus's opinion all members of a Genesis kind were intrafertile, and because he quite commonly endeavored to assign single species names to such widely spread groups (now generally called polytypic species), his name is often attached to this inclusive kind of species.

Linnaean taxonomist. A taxonomist who endeavors, in his assignment of species names, to include all individuals which can breed together. Such a taxonomist is sometimes called a "lumper."

locus (plural loci) (of a basic type or Genesis kind). In such cases the "locus of the type" refers to the form and structure (morphology) of its members. If we say "variation can proceed no farther in degree of difference than the locus of each basic type," we mean that every new generation in its appearance will belong unquestionably to the same type as its parents. Thus, to illustrate, each colt born is beyond dispute 100 percent a member of the basic horse type. Every child is, in all its morphological characters, unquestionably human. Thus the locus of each basic type consists of all the morphological characters which distinguish the horse, the man, and so on.

lumper. The taxonomist who endeavors to make his species broad enough to include all individuals which can breed together.

macroevolution. A hypothetical process which evolutionists assume enabled basic types to produce new basic types. Macroevolution is organic evolution, an assumed development of all forms of life from one, or a few, one-celled forms. Not one case is known where a basic type such as one having an apelike form produced a new basic type like a man. If macroevolution is thought of as the production by one biological species, like a variety of vinegar fly, of a new biological species of vinegar fly, then it is a demonstrable fact. However, all new biological species of vinegar flies are indisputably *still vinegar flies*. This holds for all types of plants and animals, so that macroevolution (if considered synonymous with organic evolution) has never been substantiated by the production of even one new basic type.

macroevolutionist. One who believes that complex living forms have developed naturally from simpler living forms.

mechanistic evolutionist (atheist). One who believes that in the production of living forms no other than natural forces operated. To him there is no God, and he himself is blood-related with the lower animals from whom he assumes his ancestors developed by pure chance and natural selection.

megaevolution. Synonymous with macroevolution; organic evolution.

meiosis. The process of cell division in which chromosome number is halved. Meiosis occurs when eggs and sperms are produced.

microevolution. The demonstrable production of new varieties within a basic type. This process has neither the magnitude nor the quality to produce, even in infinite time, new basic types. Because the production of new varieties within basic kinds is demonstrable, creationists accept it. Thereby, through a semantic coincidence, creationists can be called "microevolutionists."

microevolutionist. One who accepts the demonstrable fact that new varieties do develop within basic types.

min. A Hebrew root meaning "kind."

modern species. This is an indefinite expression, because some modern species have been named by splitters and are really no more than subspecies, geographic races, or varieties, while other modern species have been named by lumpers and may be so broad as to include, for example, all dogs of the world, domesticated as well as wild.

monotypic species. A species which is not divided into several

GLOSSARY

subspecies. It is sometimes referred to as a nondimensional population.

monstrosities. Forms which deviate greatly from the natural form. The geneticist Goldschmidt referred to mutant forms as "hopeful monsters" because he theorized that through them new basic types might eventually appear. However, laboratory findings give no hope of macroevolution through mutation.

morphological species. Species based entirely on form, structure, and coloration, without regard to crossability.

morphology. The branch of biology which deals primarily with the form and structure of living organisms.

multidimensional population. One which taxonomists have divided into two or more subspecies.

natural selection. The composite effect of all conditions and activities, physical as well as biological, which results in the survival of the fittest (the survival of those forms of animals and plants best adjusted to the conditions under which they live), and extinction of poorly adapted forms. This pervading effect has nothing to do with the arrival of new basic types, contrariwise merely with the types which are already on hand.

nomenclature (biological). System of names used in biology. The binomial (two names) system of nomenclature is now almost universally adopted. In this system Latin and Greek are used. The first name is that of the genus and the second that of the species. To illustrate, the scientific name of man is *Homo* (genus) *sapiens* (species). Linnaeus popularized this system.

nondimensional population. One which consists of a single species with no subspecies.

omnipotent. All powerful.

omnipresent. Everywhere present.

omniscient. All knowing.

organic evolution. Synonymous with macroevolution. The assumed development of complex forms from simple forms. There is no empirical evidence (laboratory proof) that this magnitude of change is, or ever was, possible in nature.

ornithologist. One who specializes in the study of birds.

outbreeding organisms. This refers to organisms where maleness resides in one individual and femaleness in another, for example, in cats, dogs, and box elder trees. The new individual develops normally from a fertilized egg.

paleontology. The scientific study of fossil animals and plants.
parallelism of form. See "law of convergence."
parthenogenesis. The development from eggs without fertilization. This phenomenon is found among many crustaceans, rotifers, certain orders of insects such as the Hymenoptera (example: ichneumon wasp), and plant lice. It is fairly common among plants, such as the dandelion.
phenomenon (natural). Any fact or event of a scientific interest susceptible of scientific description and explanation.
phenotype. The external appearance of a plant or an animal as distinguished from its genetic make-up.
phylogenetic system. A classification system assumedly based on the race history of a plant or an animal.
phylum. See "classification categories."
physiological isolating mechanisms. Chemical changes, possibly occurring in the genes as mutations, which result in the appearance of an individual that cannot mate with other members of the population.
physiological species. Synonymous with biological species. A population of similar organisms which are interfertile.
physiology. The science of the functions of body organs.
plankton. Minute water plants and animals which cannot significantly move themselves, so are dependent upon such external agents as currents. They are thus floating organisms which drift as acted upon by the environment.
ploidy. A shortening of "polyploidy."
polyploidy. Cases in which the chromosome number is a multiple of the basic haploid (one member of each chromosome pair) number. All multiples higher than the normal number 2n (where "n" is the haploid number), are polyploid. Triploid, tetraploid, hexaploid, and octaploid are instances of polyploidy. Polyploid series are common in some genera of plants but rare in animals.
polytypic species. A species which contains two or more subspecies.
population (as used in ecology). A group of organisms of the same species occupying a particular space.
primary adaptation (as used in this book). The fitness of an organism, as that of the squirrel for the tree and of the fish for water, which was created in the organism at its first appearance during Creation week.

GLOSSARY

prototype. Synonym for "archetype."
qualitatively. As used in this book, concerned with the quality or kind of specific chemical substances.
race. Many different meanings have been assigned to this term. In the combination "geographic race" it is sometimes synonymous with "subspecies." More generally the term "race" designates populations or aggregates of populations within formally recognized subspecies. "Ecological race" designates ecologically differentiated populations. "Microgeographic race" applies to local populations.
radioactive timeclocks. Unstable inorganic substances such as uranium-238, thorium-232, and potassium-40 which, at certain known rates, by casting off alpha and beta particles, decompose into other chemical substances and finally to a stable substance, which in the case of uranium-238 is lead-206. It has been assumed that by a comparison of the quantity of the mother substance present with that of the final stable product, the age of the mineral containing the "clock" can be found. Because of their dependence upon several undemonstrable assumptions, these data hardly qualify as true scientific evidence. The organic radioactive clock carbon-14 is used to compare ages of organic materials assumed to be less than some thirty to fifty thousand years old. Again the assumptions involved cast considerable question on the accuracy of datings which would suggest ages beyond the possibility of historical checks.
recessive (genetic character). The character which is masked when the dominant gene of its alternate character is present.
recombination. This occurs when genes already present in certain combinations may through segregation and fertilization be united in new combinations, producing new characters.
reproductive gap. The factor which prevents individuals in one kind of population from crossing with individuals of another kind in a given area.
reproductively isolated. The condition occurring when a reproductive gap is present. Even if cohabitation occurred, hybrids would not be produced, because, apparently, a chemical incompatibility exists between the germ cells of one kind when meeting germ cells of another kind.
resolution. Under magnification in optics, the act or property of rendering visible the separate parts of an object.

reversion (atavism). In crosses in which one parent brings in a dominant which the other lacks, an ancestral color, for example, will appear which neither parent showed. Thus if a black rat (genotype aaRR) is crossed with a yellow rat (genotype AArr), the first generation hybrids (genotype AaRr) are gray in color like the ancestral wild rats.

scholastics (schoolmen). Teachers in the medieval universities.

secondary adaptation. An expression used in this book to indicate the more or less minor adjustments made by organisms since Creation.

semantics. The meaning and use of words.

sexual forms. Those organisms in which reproduction is accomplished through the fusion of sexual cells, an egg with a sperm.

special creation. The doctrine of origins which holds that the first two chapters of Genesis are literally true in their portrayal of a literal Creation week, in which all basic kinds of organisms were created by fiat command of God. Accordingly the basic kinds would have no genetic relation one with the other.

species. A taxonomic group representing the smallest number of individuals of all such groups. See "classification categories" above.

speculative. Involving, or formed by, speculation; theoretical; not established by demonstration.

speculative science. Science consists of two parts: demonstrable facts, and speculative items, those not at present demonstrable. The latter items, being subjective, can be explained, often with equal logic, from at least two points of view. For example, does the presence of a vertebral column in many animals indicate blood relationship through evolution or the use of an archetype by a Creator who employed the column, modifying it in various ways and thus producing different forms which are unrelated genetically?

splitter species. "Species" which are actually no more than subspecies, races, or breeds of a true polytypic species.

splitter taxonomist. A taxonomist who employs only morphological characters in naming organisms and thus often assigns species names to populations which are only subspecies or even lower categories.

spontaneous generation. The assumption that living creatures may arise naturally from nonliving matter.

GLOSSARY

subspecies. An aggregate of local populations of a species, inhabiting a geographic subdivision of the range of the species, and differing taxonomically from other populations of the species (Mayr).

sympatric species. Populations the individuals of which are within cruising range of each other during the breeding season, even though the habitats in which they occur do not overlap in space.

synthesists. Evolutionist biologists who believe that new basic types were eventually produced through observable variation and sorting of the variants by natural selection.

systematic unit. One of the main categories in classification. For the categories see "classification categories."

taxonomic. Pertaining to the laws and principles of the classification of organisms into what are thought to be natural relationships.

taxonomic categories. Synonymous with "classification categories."

taxonomist. One who classifies plants and animals.

taxonomy. Synonymous with "classification."

tetraploid. Cells having four times the basic chromosome number, ie, twice the diploid number.

tetrapods. Members of the superclass Tetrapoda: Amphibia, Reptilia (when four-footed), Aves, and Mammalia.

theistic evolutionist. See "evolution."

throwbacks. An organism which reverts to an ancestral type of character. See "reversion (atavism)."

transcendent. Escapes classification in any accepted category. Goes beyond what is given or presented in experience and knowledge. This term applies to the Supreme Being.

translocation. A situation within a cell nucleus where a piece of one chromosome becomes broken off and attached to another chromosome, often of another pair. More common are reciprocal translocations where there is an exchange of parts by nonhomologous (not in the same chromosome pair) chromosomes.

transmutation (in biology). An assumed change of one basic type of organism into another, ie, organic evolution. Evolution of this sort has never been demonstrated.

transpecific evolution. Synonymous with "macroevolution."

trilobites. A marine animal probably allied with the crustaceans, now found only in fossil form.

variation (in biology). In an organism, divergence in structural or physiological characters from those typical or usual in the group (especially the species) to which it belongs. Also, the concrete result or effect of such a divergence, especially an organism differing from a type, or from its parents.

variety (in biology). Linnaeus used the term "variety" for all populations less than a species. In 1758 he recognized six varieties under *Homo sapiens: Americanus, Europaeus, Asiaticus, Afer,* and two others which are monstrosities or mythical. During the last 100 years the use of the term "variety" has gradually diminished in zoology until its abandonment for geographic races is nearly complete. A similar movement in botany has not achieved unanimous acceptance (Mayr). At the present time the term "variety" has largely given way in zoology to the term "subspecies."

volcanism. As used in physical geography and geology, the term includes natural processes resulting in the formation of volcanoes, lava fields, and other volcanic phenomena.

REFERENCES

Chapter 1
1. R. A. Pimental, "Mendelian infraspecific divergence levels and their analysis." *Systematic Zoology* 8:139-159.
2. Griffith Taylor, *Environment and Race* (London: Oxford University Press, 1926).
3. Theodosius Dobzhansky, "Further Data on the Variation of the Y Chromosome in Drosophila Pseudoobscura," *Genetics* 22:340-346.
4. Richard Goldschmidt, *The Material Basis of Evolution* (New Haven, Conn.: Yale University Press, 1940), p. 8.

Chapter 2
1. John Ray, *Historia Plantarum Generalis*, vol. 1 (London, 1686).
2. Carolus Linnaeus, *Classes Plantarum* (Leyden, 1738).
3. ———, *Systema Naturae*, 10th ed. (Stockholm, 1758).
4. United States Department of Agriculture, *Yearbook of Agriculture*, 1936, pp. 183-193.
5. Linnaeus, *Systema Naturae*.
6. ———, *Systema Vegetabilium*, 13th ed. (Gottingen, Germany: J. C. Dietrich, 1774).
7. Ernst Mayr, *Animal Species and Evolution* (Cambridge, Mass.: Harvard University Press, Belknap Press, 1963), p. 4.
8. Charles Darwin, *The Origin of Species*, 6th ed., Everyman's Library 811 Science (New York: E. P. Dutton and Co., 1958), pp. 54, 59.
9. Mayr, *The Species Problem* (Washington, DC: American Association for the Advancement of Science, no. 50, 1957), p. 2.
10. Raymond E. Hall and Keith R. Kelson, *The Mammals of North America* (New York: Ronald Press Co., 1959), vol. 2, pp. 843-846.
11. *Ibid.*, 855-859.
12. A. H. Sturtevant and G. W. Beadle, *An Introduction to Genetics* (Philadelphia: W. B. Saunders Co., 1939), p. 149. See also U.S. Department of Agriculture *Yearbook*, 1936, pp. 490, 491.
13. Ernest P. Walker et al, *Mammals of the World* (Baltimore: The Johns Hopkins Press, 1964), vol. 2, pp. 1429-1431.

Chapter 3
1. Theodosius Dobzhansky, "A Critique of the Species Concept in Biology," *Philosophicae Science* 2:244, 245.
2. Ernst Mayr, "Speciation Phenomena in Birds," *American Naturalist* 74:249-278.
3. ———, *Principles of Systematic Zoology* (New York: McGraw-Hill, 1969).
4. George G. Simpson, "Criteria for Genera, Species, and Subspecies in Zoology and Paleozoology," *Annals of the New York Academy of Science* 44:145-178.
5. Dobzhansky, "Mendelian Populations and Their Evolution." *American Naturalist*, 84:401-418.
6. Dobzhansky, *Genetics of the Evolutionary Process* (New York: Columbia University Press, 1970), p. 354 (hereafter cited as *G. Ev. Process*).
7. V. Grant, *The Origin of Adaptations* (New York: Columbia University Press, 1963).
8. J. S. Huxley, *The New Systematics* (Oxford: Clarendon Press, 1940).
9. Hall and Kelson, *The Mammals of North America*, vol. 2, pp. 855-859.
10. Mayr, *Animal Species*, pp. 340-341.
11. *Ibid.*, p. 341.
12. ———, *Systematics and the Origin of Species* (New York: Columbia University Press, 1942), p. 114.
13. Dobzhansky, *Genetics and the Origin of Species*, 2d ed. (New York: Columbia University Press, 1941), pp. 307-314 (hereafter cited as *G. O. Species*).
14. Mayr, *Systematics*, p. 204.
15. Dobzhansky, and Carl Epling,

Contributions to the Genetics, Taxonomy, and Ecology of Drosophila Pseudoobscura and Its Relatives (Washington, DC; Carnegie Institution, no. 554, 1944), p. 6.
16. ———, "Complete Reproductive Isolation Between Two Morphologically Similar Species of Drosophila," *Ecology* 27 (July 1946): 205.
17. *Ibid.*, p. 209.
18. *Ibid.*
19. Annie F. Gray, *Mammalian Hybrids* (Farnham Royal, Bucks, England: Commonwealth Agricultural Bureaux, 1954).
20. ———, *Bird Hybrids* (Farnham Royal: Commonwealth, 1958).
21. G. Ledyard Stebbins, Jr, *Variation and Evolution in Plants* (New York: Columbia University Press, 1950), p. 64.
22. *Gray's Manual of Botany*, 8th ed. (New York: American, 1950), pp. 706, 707.
23. Frank L. Marsh, *Fundamental Biology* (Lincoln, Neb.: author-publisher, 1941), p. 100. See also *idem.*, *Evolution, Creation, and Science*, rev. ed. (Washington, DC: Review and Herald, 1947), pp. 174, 175; *idem.*, *Studies in Creationism* (Wash.: Review, 1950), pp. 248, 249.
24. Jacques Loeb, *The Mechanistic Conception of Life* (Chicago: University of Chicago Press, 1912).
25. Dobzhansky, *G. Ev. Process*, pp. 410-414.
26. Mary C. Weiss and Howard Green, "Human-mouse Hybrid Cell Lines Containing Partial Components of Human Chromosomes and Functioning Human Genes," *Proceedings of the National Academy of Sciences* (U.S.A.) 58, no. 3 (September 1967): 1104-1111.
27. Daniel Rabovsky, "Molecular Biology: Gene Insertion Into Mammalian Cells," *Science*, 26 November 1971, pp. 933, 934.
28. Richard Goldschmidt, *The Material Basis of Evolution* (New Haven, Conn.: Yale University Press, 1940), p. 8.

Chapter 4

1. E. W. Sinnot, L. C. Dunn, and T. Dobzhansky, *Principles of Genetics*, 5th ed. (New York: McGraw-Hill, 1958), p. 11.
2. Ariel G. Loewy and Philip Siekevitz, *Cell Structure and Function* (New York: Holt, Rinehart and Winston, 1963).
3. Dobzhansky, *G. Ev. Process*, pp. 17, 18.
4. Gordon Rattray Taylor, *The Science of Life* (New York: McGraw-Hill, 1963), pp. 329-344.
5. Francis Crick and James Watson, "A Structure for Deoxyribose Nucleic Acid," *Scientific American*, October 1962.
6. Robert Paul Levine, *Genetics*, 2nd ed. (New York: Holt, Rinehart and Winston Inc., 1968), p. 177.
7. Dobzhansky, *G. Ev. Process*, p. 35.
8. Levine, p. 28.

Chapter 5

1. Levine, *Genetics*, p. 154.
2. Dobzhansky, *G. Ev. Process*, p. 72.
3. *Ibid.*, pp. 78, 79.
4. ———, *G. O. Species*.
5. P. L. Altman and Dorothy S. Dittmer, Comps., *Handbook of Biological Data: Growth, Including Reproduction and Morphological Development* (Washington, DC: Federation of American Societies for Experimental Biology, 1962), pp. 1-5.
6. A. Muntzing, "The Evolutionary Significance of Autopolyploidy," *Hereditas* 21:270-277.
7. Edgar Anderson and K. Sax, "A Cytological Monograph of the American Species of Tradescantia," *Botanical Gazette* 97, no. 3 (March 1936): 433-476.
8. C. L. Huskins, "The Origin of Spartina Townsendii," *Genetics* 12, no. 6 (1931): 531-538.
9. A. H. Sturtevant and G. W. Beadle, *An Introduction to Genetics* (Philadelphia: W. B. Saunders, 1939), p. 149.
10. Sinnot, Dunn, and Dobzhansky, *Principles of Genetics*, 5th ed., p. 294.
11. Dobzhansky, *G. O. Species*, p. 81.
12. David Lack, *Darwin's Finches*, Harper Torchbooks: The Science Library (New York: Harper, 1939), p. 15.
13. *Ibid.*, p. 4.

Chapter 6

1. Charles C. Hurst, *The Mechanism of Creative Evolution* (Cambridge, England: Cambridge University Press, 1932), p. 159.
2. *Journal of Heredity* 7 (November 1916): 504.
3. Hurst, pp. 166, 167.

4. *Ibid.*, p. 135.
5. *Ibid.*, pp. 140, 141.
6. Samuel G. Morton, "Hybridity in Animals and Plants," a paper read before the Academy of Natural Sciences in Philadelphia, November 4 and 11, 1846. Published in *American Journal of Science and Arts* 3 (2d series, 1847): 7.
7. *Livestock Journal*, London, Jan. 16, 1931, p. 72.
8. *Consumer's Guide*, vol. 9, no. 12, p. 83 (November 1943).
9. Gray, *Bird Hybrids.*
10. Loeb, *The Mechanistic Conception of Life*, 1912.
11. *Yearbook of Agriculture*, 1936, p. 183.
12. Edward C. Colin, *Elements of Genetics*, 2d ed. (Philadelphia: Blackiston, 1946), pp. 222, 223.
13. Frank L. Marsh, "The Genesis Kinds and Hybridization: Has Man Ever Crossed With Any Animal?" *Creation Research Society Quarterly* 10, no. 1 (June 1973): 31-37.
14. Dobzhansky, *G. O. Species, p. 299.*
15. *Ibid.*, pp. 302, 303.
16. Goldschmidt, *The Material Basis of Evolution*, p. 127.

Chapter 7
1. Chester A. Arnold, *An Introduction to Paleobotany* (New York: McGraw-Hill, 1947), p. 7.
2. William C. Darrah, *Principles of Paleobotany* (New York: Ronald Press, 1960), p. 39.
3. Henry N. Andrews, *Studies in Paleontology* (New York: John Waley and Sons, 1961), p. 401.
4. T. G. Tutin, "Phylogeny of Flowering Plants; Fact or Fiction," *Nature*, January 26, 1952, p. 126.
5. Austin H. Clark, *The New Evolution: Zoogenesis* (Baltimore: Williams and Wilkins, 1930), pp. 100, 101.
6. James R. Beerbower, *Search for the Past* (Edgewood Cliffs, N.J.: Prentice-Hall, 1960), pp. 424, 467, 469, 472.
7. Alfred S. Romer in *Genetics, Paleontology, and Evolution*, ed. Glenn Jepsen, Ernst Mayr, and G. G. Simpson (Princeton, N.J.: Princeton University Press, 1949), p. 114.

8. Norman D. Newell, "The Nature of the Fossil Record," *Proceedings of the American Philosophical Society* 103, no. 2 (April 23, 1959): 103.
9. Dwight D. Davis in *Genetics, Paleontology, and Evolution*, pp. 74, 77.
10. George G. Simpson, *Tempo and Mode in Evolution* (New York: Columbia University Press, 1944), p. 115.
11. ———, *The Major Features of Evolution* (New York: Columbia University Press, 1953), p. 360.
12. ———, *Tempo and Mode in Evolution*, p. 99.
13. G. Brent Dalrymple and James G. Moore, "Argon 40: Excess in Submarine Pillow Basalts From Kilauea Volcano, Hawaii," *Science* 161, no. 3846 (September 13, 1968): 1132-1135.
14. C. S. Noble and J. J. Naughton, "Deep-ocean Basalts: Inert Gas Content and Uncertainties in Age Dating," *Science* 162, no. 3850 (October 11, 1968): 265, 266.

Chapter 9
1. G. H. M. Lawrence, *An Introduction to Plant Taxonomy* (New York: Macmillan, 1955), pp. 9, 10.
2. Erik Nordenskiold, *The History of Biology* (New York: Tudor, 1928), p. 463.
3. Dobzhansky, *G. O. Species*, pp. 302, 303.
4. Dobzhansky and Epling, *Contributions to the Genetics*, p. 6.
5. G. A. Kerkut, *Implications of Evolution* (New York: Pergamon Press, 1960), p. 154.
6. Ruth Moore and the Editors of *Life, Evolution* (New York: Time 1962); Sir Gavin de Beer, *Atlas of Evolution* (New York: Thomas Nelson and Sons 1964).
7. Horatio H. Newman, *Evolution, Genetics, and Eugenics*, 3d ed. (Chicago: University of Chicago Press, 1932), pp. 54, 55.
8. *Ibid.*, p. 55.
9. *Ibid.*, p. 366.
10. *Ibid.*, p. 57.
11. Lack, *Darwin's Finches* (Harper Torchbooks. The Science Library. Harper Brothers, 1939); Moore, *Evolution*, pp. 30, 31.
12. E. D. Dodson, *A Textbook of Evolution* (Philadelphia: W. B. Saunders, 1952), p. 38.

13. Newman, p. 73.
14. W. C. Allee and Karl P. Schmidt, *Ecological Animal Geography*, 2d ed. (New York: John Wiley and Sons, 1951), pp. 642, 643; Carl Eigenmann, *Cave Vertebrates of America* (Washington, DC: Carnegie Institution, no. 104, 1909).

Chapter 10

1. A. V. Yablokov, *Variability of Mammals*. Translated from the Russian (New Delhi: Amerind Publishing Co. Available from the National Technical Information Service, Springfield, Va.), xxi, 350 pp. Illustrated.
2. R. J. Berry, and H. N. Southern (eds), *Variation in Mammalian Populations*. Symposium of the Zoological Society of London. No. 26. 403 pp. Published for the Zoological Society by Academic Press, Berkeley Square House, Berkeley Square, London. WIX 6 BA.
3. Hilbert R. Siegler, *Evolution or Degeneration–Which?* (Milwaukee: Northwestern Publishing House, 1972), pp. 38-41; book review of same by Frank L. Marsh in *Creation Research Society Quarterly* 10, no. 2 (September 1973): 125-127.

INDEX

adaptations, primary 113
  secondary 113
adaptive radiation 112
  never been demonstrated to result in new basic types 112
Aesculus carnea, pink-flowered horse chestnut, a hybrid from white parents 69
allopolyploidy 55-59
American eel, varies only slightly 9
analogous structures 108, 109
archetypes, Linnaeus's theory of 115
  limited in application 115
  must the Creator have used them in all cases? 115, 116
Ascaris, has only two chromosomes in each cell 43
autopolyploidy 55, 56

bara, Hebrew: "create" 36, 97, 99
baramin, an acceptable classification category because so easily recognized 38-40
  consists of all individuals among whom true fertilization is possible 38
  distinguished through morphology and crossability 39, 40
  name suggested for Genesis kind in 1941 by Marsh 36, 102, 121
basic type, every, in existence by close of sixth day of Creation week 87, 88, 100
basic types, no new, appeared after close of Day Six 100
  originated at beginning of life on earth at Creation 18
beans, variants of 9
behemah, Hebrew for domestic animals 97
Bible knows nothing about organic evolution 122
biblical portrayal of kinds as self-reproducing units 16
biological species, based on reproductive gap between clusters 26
  defined 32
  defined by, Dobzhansky 26
    Mayr 26
    Simpson 26
  first and last physiological 33
  gene pool concept 26
  recognition of, marks great advance in

biology 27
  trend among evolutionists toward acceptance of 26
  undistinguished everywhere except in breeding pen 33
biologists, divided into two camps over objectivity of species 20
bison, American and European 15
Bonellia, difference in appearance of male and female 16
Bonnet, a creationist, first to use the word "evolution" 11

Canis latrans, coyote 30
C. lupus, gray wolf 30
cattalo, bison-cow hybrid 35, 78
categories, present taxonomic, quite arbitrary 121
cattle, breeds among 105
  illustrate splitter species 23
  may constitute descendants of a single Genesis kind 31
cats and dogs or rabbits cannot cross 70, 71
chalcid wasps, vary only slightly in each population 9
change, greatest observable, is mere production of variants within existing basic groups 64
  processes of, have not erased discontinuity 64, 65
chayyath há áres, Hebrew for "wild beasts of the earth" 98
Christ accepted Genesis as historically true 122
chromosomal aberrations 54-66
chromosomal changes, deletions 61
  duplications 61
  even in its greatest effect, nothing basically new is produced 62, 63
  inversions 61-63
  mutations 54-66
  serve to cause cross-sterility among members of a Genesis kind 75, 76
  translocations 61, 62
chromosome numbers in typical animals and plants 43, 54
chromosomes, animals with same number as in man 54
  of male may in "hybrids" be cast out in early embryonic stages 37
classification, essential for convenience of reference to any organism 7, 8
  its significance to the creationist 8

to the mechanistic or atheistic
evolutionist 8
to the theistic evolutionist 8
complex from simple never demonstrated 10
corn, breeds among 105
variants of 9
cows, variants of 9
created kind, distinguishable in museum as well as in field 33
first morphological but lastly physiological 33
creation of basic types, only a few thousand years ago 118
creation, of large types and possibly also of subordinate groups 87, 90
special, original kinds distinguished by similar morphology and sterility 121
creationist, by definition a "microevolutionist" 111
creationists and evolutionists accept all demonstrable facts 24, 119
creationists, assume no genetic relationship between basic types of organisms 118
commonly display little interest on present status of the Genesis kind 34
consider whole forest of trees as representative of "tree of life" 115
dissatisfied with terms "micro-" and "macroevolution" 11
many hold that Genesis kinds never could cross 28
not unified on opinion of status of created kinds in nature today 34
progressive (see Glossary)
special 118
vary in concept of reproductive behavior of Genesis kinds 27, 28
Creator, apparently takes delight in variation of compatible forms 117
cannot be charged with trickery in creation of basic types 106

Darwin, Charles, confused disproof of scholastic interpretation with disproof of Genesis 18, 19
could trace migration of animals because no new kinds developed 19
developed theory of minute variations winnowed by natural selection 20
did not disprove Genesis 104
fixed his attention at too low a taxonomic level 17
principal service to science was publicizing the fact of variation 17
successfully promoted the idea of organic evolution 19
thought species arbitrary units 20
thought variation among living things contrary to Genesis 104

Darwin's finches 65, 66
Darwin's observations in complete harmony with Genesis and natural facts 104
deletions, chromosomal 61
deshe, Hebrew, "to be damp" (Genesis 1:11, 12) 93
discontinuity, basis for classification 7
dooms evolutionist "tree of life" 115
in living and fossil nature, greatest single roadblock against organic evolution 120
no process of change can bridge 64
occurrence of sharply different populations 7, 8
of diversity 8, 101
DNA, deoxyribonucleic acid 44-48
does not undergo continual metabolism 45, 46
has the required characteristics of hereditary material 46
its physical structure 46
or gene, different possible sequences of pairs of nucleotides in, is immense 48
story of its discovery 46
synonymous with gene 45
Dobzhansky, defines biological species 26
defines microevolution and macroevolution 35
first geneticist to define the biological species 26
Drosophila, vinegar fly, a genus rich in morphologically similar species 32, 33
equinoxialis and *D. willistoni* morphologically indistinguishable 33, 75
illustrates difference between biological species and Genesis kind 40
persimilis, illustrates difference between biological species and Genesis kind 39, 40
species name given to race B of *D. pseudoobscura* 32
pseudoobscura, races A and B 32, 75
duplications, chromosomal 61

entities, only two in living world, the individual and the basic type 121
ets peri, Hebrew for "trees of fruit" (Genesis 1:11, 12) 93
eseb, Hebrew for "herbage" (Genesis 1:11, 12) 93
evolution, books on, filled with examples of microevolution only 107
has become an obsession to evolutionists 106
organic, teaches that first life appeared on this earth at least 600 million years ago 118
suggests development of new basic

types 11
evolutionists, in search for basic unit fix
 attention at too low a level 40
 marshal examples of microevolution in
  effort to prove macroevolution 105

fertilization, a concrete test for the
 Genesis kind 103
 true, chromosome groups of both parents join in formation of early blastomeres 37
fishes, blind cave 116
fixity, among living things 103, 104
 of kinds, one of biology's most
  important principles 106
Flood, evidences of 86, 87
form and structure, basis of all
 classification systems attempted
  so far 113
 similar, does not necessarily indicate
  genetic relationship 107
Formenkreis 29
fossil-bearing layers, known to extend
 down at least 25,000 feet 80
fossils, can neither refute nor prove
 evolution or special creation 83
 claimed by reputable evolutionists to
  constitute only real proof for
  evolution 80
 classified by same characters as are
  living relatives 82
 connecting links among, cannot be
  demonstrated 101, 102
 just as complex at earliest appearance
  as relatives are today 64
 nature of evidence on, such that
  student can believe or reject any
  item 84
 of most rock layers represent
  organisms which all lived at one
  time 85
 record of, in harmony with the Genesis
  account of origins and the Flood
  84
 truth about them comes as a shock to
  most evolutionists 84
fox, red, illustrates use once made of
 minute morphological differences
 21, 22, 29
fur-fowl in Indiana, false report of 70

gene, chemical make-up of 43, 44
gene mutations 51-54
 biochemical 53
 lethal 53
 probably a change at level of one or
  two nucleotides 51, 52
 visible 52
gene, chemistry of, determines
 morphology 16
 each, has sole function of building one
  specific protein 47
Genesis states, land animals migrated
  outward from mountains of
  Ararat 18
 only that plants brought forth after
  their kinds 88
 on Day Six God ended His work of
  creating new kinds 89
 repeatedly that plants and animals
  were created after their kinds
  88, 89
Genesis teaches fixity because kinds
 were created and kinds do not
 change 90
Genesis kinds, and modern biological
 species identical in many cases 91
 by their continuity 102
 easily distinguished, by morphological
  characters 34
 not identifiable with any one
  taxonomic category today 34
geologic time, can be proven or
 disproven only by inference 81
ginkgo, varies only slightly from fossil
 form to living form 9
God must be somewhat anthropomorphic because man was
 created in His image 98
Goldschmidt states microevolution does
 not explain macroevolution 10, 11

haploidy 54, 55
hereditary material, its location in the
 organism 43, 44
heteroploidy 54, 59, 60, 62, 63
hinny 78
Holy Scriptures know no derivative type
 of origin of new kinds 94
homologous structures 110
horses, variants of 9, 14
Huxley, Julian, suggested the names
 "monotypic" and "polytypic" 29
hybrids, examples of, close crosses
 among animals 78
 close crosses among plants 78, 79
 widest crosses among animals
  77, 78
 widest crosses among plants 78
 produced only between organisms
  close together in taxonomic
  lists 79
hybridization 67-79
 between groups within one Genesis
  kind sometimes cannot occur 72,
  74, 75
 cannot occur between members of two
  basic types 71, 72
 experiments on, of great value in
  discovering Genesis kinds 74
 largest possible effects of, are microevolution only 69
 may extend over taxonomic groups in
  commonly unexpected ways 73
 narrow and wide 67
 occurs only among organisms which
  are members of the same basic

147

type 79
 of man with any other animal never
  known to occur 73
 past records of, very often untrue 69
 sources of a large portion of variation
  due to new recombinations 67, 79
 source of new species 68, 69

intratypal species (see Glossary)
inversions, chromosomal 61-63
isolating mechanisms may develop new
 intratypal clusters, not new basic
 types 76, 77

Jordan, French botanist who pioneered
 assignment splitter species names
 22
Jordanian species 22

kianager, of kiang-onager hybrid 78
kinds, bring forth only after their kinds
 89, 90, 108
 new not formed 9
kinship, close, a general indication of
 similar morphology 108
Kleinschmidt, first to point out difference
 between Linnaean and polytypic
 species 28
 suggested calling large natural unit
 Formenkreis 28, 29

laboratory proof, none coercive with
 regard to origins 118
liger, lion-tiger hybrid 78
Linnaean species 22
Linnaeus, Carolus, as a lumper 15, 22
 as a special creationist 15
 as a splitter 15
 first to recognize reproductive gap 25
 his mature opinion of created units 16
 his theory of archetypes 115
 his understanding of species 15, 16
 known as father of modern
  taxonomy 14
 positive influence of, toward
  constancy and objectivity of
  species 16, 17
Loeb found incorrect in assumption that
 all marine teleost fish will hybridize 37, 72
logic, necessary when conceiving of
 macroevolution, to leave the realm
 of reality 113
logical extension of a natural fact, may
 not be biological 107, 108
lumper, species 28
 taxonomists 22

macroevolution 10, 11, 13, 28, 63
 defined by creationists 120

is hypothetical or make-believe only
 11, 12, 113
 needs clearer definition by
  evolutionists 40, 41
 not one illustration of, can be found 23
 man, physically similar to animals 99
marsh grass 57, 58
Mayr, cites frequency of polytypic
  species 30, 31
 defines biological species 26
 thought no conflict between evolution
  and objective species 20
men, 160 distinct breeds of 9
microevolution 10, 11, 13, 28, 63
 at most can produce only Jordanian
  species 22
 cannot be extrapolated to
  macroevolution 106, 107
 defined by creationists 120
 by Dobzhansky 10
 examples of, surround us 10
Microevolution and macroevolution
 hang upon the definition of
 species 12
min, an imprecise word 87, 103
 Hebrew for "kind" 36, 102, 103
monotypic species 29
mule, horse-ass hybrid 78
multidimensional species: pocket
 gopher, red fox, deer mouse 29
mutations, chromosomal 54-66

natural forces and principles do not
 change through time 77
natural processes cannot bridge
 discontinuity between kinds 64
Noah's Flood accompanied by
 destruction of earth's crust to
 great depth 86
nonhereditary variations 49

origins, alternate viewpoints on, should
 be respected 122
 only two principal theories of 118

paleontologists, admissions of 80-84
paleontology has not revealed that truly
 primitive forms once lived 94
parthenogenetic development, eggs
 develop without aid of sperm 72
Passerella melodia, song sparrow, a
 polytypic species 31
Peromyscus maniculatus, deer mouse 29
phenotype, necessarily result of
 interaction of genotype and
 environment 50
phylogenetic diagrams used to portray
 assumed evolutionist origins 114
physiological characters, if compatible,
 are commonly accompanied by
 quite similar morphological
 characters 79

plants, basic types of, make evolution impossible 94
scattering of hybrid production through categories 36
ploidy 54-60
polyploidy 54-60
  systemic effect of 56, 57
polytypic species 28, 29
  geographical races 28, 29, 30
  not synonymous with Genesis kinds in all cases 30
  universal phenomenon among plants and animals 30, 31
population of biological species compared with that of Genesis kind 33
populations, multidimensional and nondimensional 29
principle, greatest biological, no basic type can produce a new basic type 122
purslane, varies only slightly 9

radioactive time clocks, merely show a diminishing age from bottom to top in sedimentary rocks 84, 85
reliability of, challenged by lava flows 85
Raphanobrassica, radish-cabbage hybrid 35, 57
Ray, John, his understanding of species 13, 22
recombinations 51
remes, Hebrew for "to move lightly" 97
Rensch, suggested polytypic species be called *Rassenkreis* 29
resemblance, degree of, commonly depends upon blood relationship 109
  physical, evolutionist says, results from genetic relationship or "convergence" 109, 110
RNA, ribonucleic acid 44-48

Santa Gertrudis, ox-Brahman hybrid 23, 78
science, consists of demonstrable portion and a speculative portion 23, 24, 119
scientist, if sincere will not refuse hypothesis until measured by demonstrable facts 19
  must distinguish between what is demonstrable and what merely subjective 24
  who accepts Genesis owes no apology 66
Simpson, defines biological species 26
"skvader," false report of hare-capercaillie cross 70
Spartina townsendii, marsh grass 57, 58
special creation teaches originally created kinds distinguished by intersterility between kinds 121
species, as understood by John Ray 13
  biological 28
  confusion of definition for 13
  lumper 28
  monotypic 29
  polytypic 28, 29
  reputable-taxonomist 28
  splitter 28
  transmutation of 14
spiderworts 56
splitter taxonomists, illustrated, by classification of red fox 21, 22
  in classification of corn 22
spontaneous generation, taught to be a natural fact 99
student of origins must think his way carefully 41
swoose, cross between swan and goose 78
syllogism (true or false?), the origin of *Drosophila persimilis* 40

taxonomic, groups listed 8
  lists hold many types of species 21, 22
taxonomists, have not produced a truly phylogenetic system 95
  looking for standard yardstick for species 25
  opinion of, regarding species still widely accepted 20, 21
theologians, of Cambridge apparently missed Genesis 8:17 104
  of Middle Ages, rendered great disservice to biology 17
  taught spontaneous generation 99
thistle butterfly, varies only slightly 9
Thomomys ubrinus, pocket gopher 29
tiglon, tiger-lion hybrid 78
time, evolutionist appeals for 66
Tradescantia, spiderworts 56
translocations, chromosomal 61, 62
transmutation of species 14
  disproved by Linnaeus 14
Triticum and *Aegilops,* goat grass 58, 59

variants, new, only new population within existing basic type 36
variation, one of most universal of facts 7
  probably occurs among all living things 7
  processes of, can never produce new basic types 105
  results from many factors in many combinations 7
  understood, the greater the harmony between special creation and demonstrable facts 120
variations, continuous series of, between markedly different variants not found 7
  hereditary 51-66
  nonhereditary (environmental,

nongenetic) and hereditary
  (genetic) 50
variety, the spice of life 7
Vulpes fulva, red fox 21, 22
  example of polytypic species 29

wheat, chromosome numbers in hybrid
  groups of 58

zebroid, zebra-horse hybrid 76

www.ingramcontent.com/pod-product-compliance
Lightning Source LLC
Chambersburg PA
CBHW070914160426
43193CB00011B/1457